Hope against Hope

*Johann Baptist Metz and Elie Wiesel
Speak Out on the Holocaust*

Studies in Judaism and Christianity

Exploration of Issues in the Contemporary Dialogue Between Christians and Jews

Editor in Chief for
Stimulus Books
Helga Croner

Editors
Lawrence Boadt, C.S.P.
Helga Croner
Rabbi Leon Klenicki
Rev. Dr. John Koenig
Kevin A. Lynch, C.S.P.
Dennis McManus
Dr. Susan Shapiro

A STIMULUS BOOK

Hope against Hope

*Johann Baptist Metz and Elie Wiesel
Speak Out on the Holocaust*

by
Ekkehard Schuster and
Reinhold Boschert-Kimmig

translated by J. Matthew Ashley

A STIMULUS BOOK
PAULIST PRESS ✦ NEW YORK ✦ MAHWAH, N.J.

We thank Leon Klenicki, Director of the Department of Interfaith Affairs of the Anti-Defamation League, for his recommendation to translate this volume into English.

Cover design by Cindy Dunne

Originally published as *Trotzdem Hoffen* by Matthias-Grünewald Verlag, Germany. English translation copyright © 1999 by Paulist Press, Inc.

Library of Congress Cataloging-in-Publication Data

Schuster, Ekkehard, 1962–
    [Trotzdem hoffen. English]
    Hope against hope : Johann Baptist Metz and Elie Wiesel speak out on the Holocaust / by Ekkehard Schuster and Reinhold Boschert-Kimmig and translated by J. Matthew Ashley.
        p.   cm. — (Studies in Judaism and Christianity) (Stimulus book)
    Includes bibliographical references.
    ISBN 0-8091-3846-8
    1. Metz, Johannes Baptist, 1928– —Interviews. 2. Hope—Religious aspects—Christianity. 3. Holocaust (Christian theology) 4. Wiesel, Elie, 1928– —Interviews. 5. Hope—Religious aspects—Judaism. 6. Holocaust (Jewish theology) I. Metz, Johannes Baptist, 1928–   . II. Wiesel, Elie, 1928–   . III. Boschert-Kimmig, Reinhold. IV. Title. V. Series.
BV4638.S3413   1999
231.7´6—dc21   99–11228
                                                                                            CIP

Published by Paulist Press
997 Macarthur Boulevard
Mahwah, New Jersey 07430

www.paulistpress.com

Printed and bound in the
United States of America

CONTENTS

ABOUT THIS BOOK

Two men, two places, and virtually the same birthdate. Their backgrounds have almost nothing in common. Only an historical catastrophe, in which one stood on the side of the victims and the other grew up in the land of the perpetrators, would later bring them to rethink their respective traditions. Johann Baptist Metz, Christian, Catholic, had a sheltered German childhood before, still a child, he was sent to the battlefield in the last year of the war. Elie Wiesel, Jew, Hasid, was also sent somewhere by the Germans—into the "realm of night," where death reigns: Auschwitz.

It would take years, even decades, before the one interiorized that horror and grasped it as something that unsettled all of his questions about God and about human beings, and before the other found a literary and religious language with which to tell its story. The Christian theologian and the Jewish writer are bound together by their passion for remembrance. This remembrance is dangerous, but it bears within a saving kernel. Both their biographies and their works are bound together by the memory of human suffering, of history's victims, as well as by a suffering unto God. Neither puts any store on comfort or consolation; herein lies their importance. Hope is found only in a defiant "and yet." For, as one of them would put it, true faith is born in the very heart of despair, and as the other would say, human beings do not come to self-knowledge in that which is comforting, but in that which is unsettling.

Ekkehard Schuster   Reinhold Boschert-Kimmig
Yom ha-Shoah, 18 April, 1993

Johann Baptist Metz

JOHANN BAPTIST METZ
BIOGRAPHICAL NOTES

Johann Baptist Metz was born on August 5 1928, in the small town of Auerbach in the upper Palatinate—these seemingly banal biographical facts already bring us close to the core of Metz's theological life, his way of perceiving and thinking, of witnessing to his faith, of arguing and provoking.

Auerbach represents an "arch-Catholic" milieu and a virtually seamless religiosity, a homeland where any trace of modernity is barely discernible. To borrow an expression that Metz applies to Auerbach: you come from far away when you come from there, practically from the fringes of the Middle Ages. This may sound anecdotal, but it is of systemic importance, as it touches on the very heart of theology as it was practiced until well after the Second World War.

For Johann Baptist Metz it is crucial to pay attention to the times and places where one lives, believes, and sometimes also does theology. How else can one talk about God, touching on the things that human beings live through, doubt, and hope for? The contrast between tradition and modernity permeates Metz's life: Auerbach and the classrooms of Innsbruck and Munich, the parish in Litzeldorf where he spent his holidays, and thirty years as professor of fundamental theology in Münster. Again and again, from different perspectives, it is the precarious relationship between tradition and modernity that finds expression in Metz's thought: for example, his surprising thesis that Catholicism is a rural religion and Protestantism is a city religion; or his defense of the stories of ordinary people against the language of supposed theological experts.

Metz spent his childhood and youth during the period of

the Third Reich. Just before the end of the war, when he was sixteen, he was called up in the final draft. Here we find the event that Metz has called the "first fissure in my biography." While he was away acting as a courier, all of his comrades, sixteen-year-olds like himself, came under attack. When he returned he found all of them dead—only vacant faces were left. A wordless cry is what remained for him— here for the first time, so Metz tells us, something unreconcilable came into his life.

The second fissure, never to be closed or reconciled, bears the name of Auschwitz. The murder of millions and the ineradicable horror it engenders became for Metz the center of his theological thinking. It has left him no alternative but to radically question heretofore familiar theological ideas and paths. Why did theologians not "see" Auschwitz? How can theology deal with Auschwitz? Are theologians too detached? Is it possible that theologians know too much, without really having exposed themselves to the full scope of the problems? Later, his most important question became: What is the significance of the fact that Christianity has its origin in the faith of the people of Israel? What have been the consequences for Christianity of 1900 years of widespread anti-Judaic theology?

As a master of language, Johann Baptist Metz knows that words not only point out, but also conceal things. He breaks through the weave of words with questions: Are we disciples, or do we only believe in discipleship? Do we love, or do we only believe in love? Metz speaks in such a prophetic and zealous way; his language can be so foreign and peculiar in confronting philosophy and theology, yet that language is simple, deep and spiritual when it approaches unintelligible suffering.

Those who have not been allowed to preserve their childhood faith intact, who have not been able to ignore the unreconciled elements in their lives, and who have not given up on directing their questions to God: these are the ones with whom Johann Baptist Metz feels the greatest affinity. What binds him most closely to his teacher, Karl Rahner, is a "virtually proletarian rebellion against everything elitist and esoteric," their common conviction that, theologically speaking, the most decisive things are often said not in learned theologies, but in the sometimes virtually mute language of those who are oppressed and who suffer.

A religion which does not simply serve up answers, but rather helps unasked questions find words—would that not be a religion which takes men and women seriously? This is Johann Baptist Metz's contribution.

THE CHURCH TODAY:
BETWEEN RESIGNATION AND HOPE

Professor Metz, even someone who is not indifferent to the fate of the Christian faith and the church has to accept the fact that things are not as well as they should be in the church today. Given that a thaw has not yet truly set in from the church's wintry season, of which Karl Rahner spoke, do you still have visions and dreams for the church today?

JBM: I have given up my great dreams for the church. Yet as time goes on I have become much more deeply troubled by something I might call a widespread God crisis, a crisis of hope. We will certainly have to talk more about it. But, as far as the church goes: I need the church. Not because the Pope and the bishops want it, but because without the church a millennium-old hope would have been forgotten long ago, a hope that is so sweeping and so improbable that no one can hope it for himself or herself alone. This does not simply give the church administration a clean bill of health. It does not prohibit criticism. In no way. Here the church, those who hold office, and, of course, the people of the church as well, are judged against a decisive standard. I might put it this way: is our church such that this hope is seen and heard, and does the church enable us to be with and for others, without which we cannot have this hope? We must all hold ourselves accountable to this standard, and convenient or not, everyone must fight to make room for this hope in the church. Of course—and this is the great danger—around here the people are breaking away. But this is also true of other more "liberal" types of Christianity that many Catholic critics of the church like to dream about.

Compared to the criticism of the church that comes from the media, this sounds unusual, particularly from a theologian whose name is widely associated with a clearly critical stance.

JBM: I do not think that we should turn the focal points of ecclesial criticism presented by the media into the center of our theological critique. I will give you a recent example. Out of a nearly one-hour-long interview, all that survived were my critique (not at all original) of Roman centralism, and a point that I have been repeating for nearly fifteen years: that religious orders in the church really ought to claim for themselves the charism of chastity, and that consequently they would be the ones called to be critics of so-called priestly celibacy, since what is at stake is a radically eschatological sign. The whole context of my critique vanished, a context which pertains to something I would like to say to you here. Today there certainly is something like a widespread crisis and weariness in the church. Yet, as important as this may be, it seems to me that this crisis is secondary. In my opinion, what is going on at a deeper level is a sort of "God crisis." Perhaps I could even say: a kind of weariness with God. Of course, this God crisis is not at all easy to perceive since it often has the pretense of being religious: a God crisis, so to speak, in a religiously enthused age. If we can characterize the ecclesial crisis some decades ago with the slogan "Jesus, yes—church, no," now it is more (and in my view all the more difficult to understand) "Religion, yes—God, no." If I am right, then surely this is a radical crisis that calls for a correspondingly fundamental reflection, one that should, of course, aim at new expressions of life in the church. These cannot be guided either by the old clerical, or by the new fundamentalist, dreams for the church. It is always imperative that one be able to walk upright in order to willingly bend one's knee to pray, in order to sense that freedom which can stem from prayer. We will probably have to talk about this language of prayer later on. At any rate, it cannot simply be recited. Becoming literate in this language is not only something we ought to urge on the Third World nations—we ourselves stand in bitter need of it. If I see aright, this requires that we come to some consensus, in a base community context, concerning our faith and our discourse about God. In the not-too-distant future the overarching ecclesial structures are going to break down hereabouts, the ecclesial way of life based on concordats is going to come to an end, the winds of diaspora will blow. Then political theology's vision of the church will become important again....

Has this been your experience over the last ten years? Thinking back on how in 1980, at the German Catholic Conference, you, together with Hans Küng, talked about a base church: then it seemed like a new development. Looking back from our present perspective it seems a little like revolutionary romanticism.

JBM: Yes, this vision of a base community church, as opposed to a folk church or a bourgeois service-church,[1] was aiming for something like a "revolution from within." Hardly anything has come of it since. In the 1980 remarks that you are alluding to I probably was speaking too quickly for the life of the church around here. Only gradually have I come to see that there is probably something that is a part of life in a base church that is normally not found among us (in contrast to poor nations and to the poor churches of this world): that is, that the social, cultural elaboration of one's identity goes hand in hand with securing a believing, religious identity. Here we are all definitely socialized in a bourgeois fashion. It is too easy for Christianity to be experienced as a rather privatistic and arbitrary accessory, which a person could supposedly do without quite easily, if for example their pocketbook requires it,[2] without anything changing much. During my encounters in Latin America, moreover, the work that my friends and colleagues are doing in base communities struck me at its most powerful and most pioneering, work that begins, so to speak, "wholly from below," in that place where all rhetoric, all merely aesthetic radicalizing of the message, breaks down, where pious metaphysics sticks in one's throat, where speechless suffering prohibits one from speaking and where only being-amidst [*Dabeisein*] counts.

What do you think of attempts, especially in pastoral theology, to learn from the experience of the Latin American base church without simply wanting to copy it? There are current attempts to bridge the Atlantic under the slogan of the "new evangelization."

JBM: "New evangelization" is a big, perhaps too big a word. At any rate we must certainly bear in mind the fact that the church today not only is present all over the world but has become a world church, and that it is not least among us, in a diaspora situation. I have said many times that the church today, under the impetus of the last Council, is on the way to becoming a culturally polycentric world church. In its cultural variety, such a world church contains a store of knowledge for the various regional churches. But in a way it will also have a sort of prohibition against transposing from one to the other. That is to say, if we want to take the historical and social particularity of the local churches seriously and give due regard to their cultural dignity, then eventually we must develop a new culture to go with the one world church. I call this a new hermeneutical culture, a culture that is sensitive to and appreciative of the particularity of the individual local churches. I do not know if the new universal catechism is particularly helpful for this. I have my doubts. And they are not related to the fact that the entire structure of faith is supposed to be brought to mind in this catechism. For example, I think it is pretty foolish to think that somebody is thinking critically by objecting to the catechism because it talks about the Last Judgment—which after all is something that the Creed does too. My problems stem from the fact that this universal catechism ends up striking one as trying to deal with the transition—certainly fraught with anxiety—from an all too culturally monocentric, eurocentric church toward a culturally polycentric world church, by getting this transition back into fixed channels as quickly as possible, and to put the new realms of experience of the faith (which are difficult to survey or predict) under linguistic discipline.

To get back to your question: no, we cannot borrow from other continents the pastoral-theological imagination needed for remaking our folk church into a kind of diaspora church. This is the case even while many of the features that we have talked about in recent years under the rubric of a basic community-oriented church are still crucial, and should in no way be forgotten. How are we going to learn to think in a more "communitarian" fashion, if I may call it that without involving myself explicitly in the parallel discussions going on in the United States? How are we going to learn to develop a new idea of solidarity in our life in church and society, against the prevailing tendencies to think of our life contexts in individualist or biographical terms, and against vanquished political visions and exhausted ecclesial visions? What does it mean for this new idea of a common life that ecclesial communities are always "communities of memory"? There will only be initiatives for building up a new way of life in a diaspora church if they arise from the grass roots—that is, if they are not simply prescribed from the outside; if women's dreams for the way society is structured finally find a place and get the attention they deserve, and so on.

THEOLOGICAL INTERRUPTIONS

You once said that your theology is "on the way to a post-idealist theology." Where are you on the way to today? What tracks are you following?

JBM: Still on this way, still the same tracks. What I mean by "post-idealist" is this: a theology which is no longer permitted or expected to present its explanations of the world and its interpretations of human existence in closed, a-situational systems. It knows of no final explanations [*Letztbegründungen*], but—if you will permit me this word-play—only explanations that finally come at the end [*Zuletztbegründungen*]. The temporal factor is unavoidably in play, its message has a temporal core. Its logic is not really a logic of identity, but of non-identity. That makes it more vulnerable than classical metaphysics, than any way of thinking guided by ideas. It is based on comparatively "weak" categories like memory and narrative. In other words, or somewhat more academically: the logic of theology has an anamnestic depth structure. And it is "practical" because in formulating its concepts it can never do without the wisdom that is gained in doing. I know that all this still sounds rather abstract. It is certainly only an outline.

How do you see things differently today? The last ten years certainly must have had an effect on a theology that rightly wants to be called "post-idealist."

JBM: That's right. In the last ten years it has been particularly important for me to confront Friedrich Nietzsche and the transformation of metaphysics into psychology and aesthetics that is connected with him. For our central European intellectual culture it could probably be said that "Marx is dead; Nietzsche lives." Yet I am not of the opinion that we can simply ignore Marx, not even after the collapse of the communist systems. I would also like to underscore this because I saw relatively early, in the early seventies, that Nietzsche was emerging once again from the shadow of Marx—which covered everything at that time. What is of enduring theological significance in Karl Marx? Let us put it this way: the Jewish spirit discovered what history is; Karl Marx—and this probably has something to do with his being a Jew—dramatized this discovery in a social-critical way within European history, and in so doing made the so-called theodicy question relevant with a new clarity and sharpness. This is precisely what we must keep before us at all costs in our theology. In addition, coming to grips with ideology critique has become anything but superfluous for the work of theology today.

We find there another "interruption" of theology's stream of ideas. It is connected with the name "Auschwitz." I am convinced that this makes every Christian theology that does not want to be unveiled as a latter-day platonism or a pure idealism into a "post-Auschwitz theology."

Such convictions certainly do not come by chance. How did it happen that the horror called "Auschwitz" has become central to your thought? It took a long time for you to express these convictions—was the long silence necessary?

JBM: I have often asked myself these questions. A couple of years ago, at a symposium in Turin, I met George Steiner, who teaches at Genf and Cambridge. We discussed just this question of the all-too-long silence after the catastrophe of Auschwitz. I found his suggestion very illuminating. He said that after World War I, Germans had been able to discuss that catastrophe quite soon; even theologians were able to produce commentaries relatively quickly on the crisis connected with the collapse of bourgeois society in that war— for example, in the apocalyptic key that we find in Karl Barth's commentary on the Letter to the Romans. The catastrophe was, to be sure, tremendous, but it did not leave them speechless. With the crisis that Auschwitz stands for we have a catastrophe for humanity which has taken on such proportions that it evoked a moratorium on speaking, particularly among reasonable people. In the face of that horror nobody knows how to think or feel about it. None of this is meant to be a belated disguise for the German "incapacity to mourn." Nothing is to be glossed over by this observation.

In any event, I too became aware of the absence of Auschwitz from our theology very late, much too late. 1968 certainly brought us to a new relationship with the German past, and finally also to a deeper consciousness of the Holocaust. Thus in the early seventies I was able to ask my great teacher and friend, Karl Rahner, why it is that Auschwitz never shows up in theology, not even in his. Rahner took my uneasiness in this regard very, very seriously.

There is yet another point of view on this silence concerning Auschwitz. When after the war many people protested that they knew nothing at all about this horror, at first I took it to be lies or repression. Even when my own mother said that she too had not heard or known anything of this Nazi crime, I still kept thinking about it. Today the following seems to shed some light on it: at the time they apparently really did not know about it, primarily because they could not imagine anything so monstrous, because they thought that all the atrocities they had been hearing about were basically wartime crimes. Only gradually, after the war, did they grasp what had really happened there. Therefore, it really does not surprise me at all that people pop up from time to time who deny this horror. Rather, it surprises me that there are so few. Finally the reality of Auschwitz blows open the horizons of our experience. Since the recent "historians' debate" pretty much everyone talks about the "historicization" of National Socialism and its crimes. There is still a question in all of this for me: the question of how one can continue to bear such a catastrophe in mind, a catastrophe which again and again is in danger of eluding our sense of history. To preserve the remembrance of Auschwitz, of the Shoah, so that it never happens among us again, we need to support our consciousness with something I call an "anamnestic culture." This is the dowry of the Jewish spirit. And it is largely missing among us, both here in Germany and in Europe as a whole, since in Auschwitz this spirit was supposed to have been snuffed out once and for all.

It took a long time before I grasped the fact that Auschwitz was a deadly attack on everything that we Christians should hold sacred. I had already been struck by this awareness when in 1973 I worked on the first draft for the text of the German synodal document, "Our Hope" [*Unsere Hoffnung*]. Although it was toned down in many ways in the final document, the section entitled "For a new way of relating to the Jewish people's history of faith" contained the first clear statement on Auschwitz from our German church.

Where did my uneasiness come from? I cannot locate its origin precisely. Today I am deeply troubled that during my student days after the war I never visited the concentration camp at Flossenbürg, which is only about fifty kilometers from my home town in the Upper Palatinate. This was the camp where Dietrich Bonhoeffer was killed, not least because he raised a hue and cry for the Jews.

In your opinion, have theologians in the meantime adequately understood that we are in a "post-Auschwitz" era and cannot avoid dealing with this challenge? Do you see this challenge beginning to be taken seriously?

JBM: Naturally one should not turn Auschwitz into a sort of "negative religion" or "negative myth" for Christians. However I have been and continue to be skeptical regarding your question. There is certainly plenty of rhetoric about guilt and responsibility concerning Auschwitz in our Christian world. But if I am right it has not yet reached the roots of Christian theology. What happened in the Shoah does not just require that we revise the way Christians and Jews have related to one another down through history; rather, it calls for a revision of Christian theology. This is what my friend Jürgen Moltmann has stressed so emphatically—and correctly. Even today, does not our theology know too little of the Jew Jesus? Should not the Dead Sea Scrolls, so heatedly discussed of late, bring home to us how deeply the origins of Christianity are woven into Jewish history?

Antisemitism does not exist only as crude racism; in theology it hardly appears in that guise anymore. However, it is to be found in a much more refined, genteel form, that is, psychologically or metaphysically. Under this guise it became the Tempter of Christian theology from its very beginnings. What I am primarily thinking of are gnostic motifs and notions. Even today these are enjoying a boom, for example in theologies impregnated by depth psychology influenced by C. G. Jung.

Elie Wiesel wrote in an early essay that "in Auschwitz it was the very idea of mankind and man himself that died." This statement has been very much on our minds. Has the idea of man really died? Do you still have confidence in humanity?

JBM: In my view Elie Wiesel has carried on enlightenment and a search for truth by means of exaggeration and heightened one-sidedness. I think that this is quite legitimate. I believe that by making such statements he wants to set in motion a process and is waiting for a saving opposition. Indeed, he even said once that "The reflective Christian knows that it was not the Jewish people that died in Auschwitz, but Christianity." I understand that statement in the same way.

For many, and for many Christians, Auschwitz has slowly slipped over the horizon of their memories. But nobody escapes the anonymous consequences of this catastrophe. The theological question after Auschwitz is not only "Where was God in Auschwitz?" It is also "Where was humanity in Auschwitz?" I want to tell you what has always touched and troubled me particularly intensely about our situation "post-Auschwitz." I mean the unhappiness, the despair, of those who survived this catastrophe. So much silent unhappiness, so many suicides! Many have been shattered by their despair over humanity. How can someone who was forced to experience in Auschwitz what "man" is capable of have any faith left in man, or even—such a tremendous word—in humanity? How could one continue living in the midst of men and women? What do we know of the menace to the humanity of human beings, we who have lived with our backs turned to this catastrophe, or who were born after it? Auschwitz has also profoundly lowered the threshold of shame between human beings. Only the forgetful survive it, or those who have already successfully forgotten that they have forgotten something. But not even those get off scott-free. One cannot sin in the name of humankind as one will. Not only the individual person, but also the idea of man and of humankind is deeply vulnerable. Only a few people make the connection between Auschwitz and the present crisis in the humanities: a growing numbness regarding universal and "high" norms and values, the decline of solidarity, a clever readiness to make ourselves small in order to adapt to any situation, a growing refusal to endow the human self with any moral perspective, and so forth. Are not all of these votes of no confidence in the human person? There is not just a surface history of the human species, but a depth history as well. Has it somehow been mortally wounded by the catastrophe of Auschwitz? This is the way I read Elie Wiesel's statement.

PHILOSOPHICAL-THEOLOGICAL ENCOUNTERS— FORMATIVE FIGURES

The philosophical impetus, your view beyond, from a theological perspective: is that the mark your teacher Karl Rahner has left on you?

JBM: There is no doubt that this has to do with Karl Rahner; indeed, virtually everything in my theology has something to do with him. And this fundamentally philosophical impulse was where we were close, spontaneously close. Admittedly, I understand Hegel differently than he—and this is connected with the matters we just spoke of. For me Hegel's greatness is not so much as a philosophical system-builder but as a philosophical analyst of time. His famous statement that philosophy is time grasped in ideas is to me the most important element of Hegel's significance for theology. Nonetheless, it is almost impossible to overestimate the mark that Karl Rahner made on my theology. His influence went far beyond the academic and into the personal—it has an existential dimension for me. In a certain way he was the "father" of my faith. I think the story of my theology and the story of my faith are so interwoven, so strongly tied to one another, that the one who left a mark on my theology also played a part in the process of my own faith. Understanding theology as a way of life derives entirely from Rahner. Herbert Vorgrimler, my theological companion under Rahner, can also attest to this fact.

The theological controversies and arguments that arose subsequently also ran their course in a friendly manner. I cannot say in detail which of our differences are of biographical origin—perhaps because of my experiences during the war, the way my childhood dreams were shattered, and my subsequent experiences during the sixties. However, I am absolutely convinced that theology has to show its greatness precisely in non-identity. And Karl Rahner explicitly emphasized that he took the objections of political theology, as I have formulated them, very seriously, and considered them to be the only substantive critique of his theology. It was a distinctive mark of his character as a thinker that he opened himself to contrary views; his thinking had a unique maieutic power.

Despite the highest esteem for his theology and despite the high regard in which I hold him, I am still of the opinion that his transcendental concept is in the final analysis ahistorical, too far removed from history. Considered from the perspective of systematic theology, the apocalyptic or eschatological play a major role for me; even Christology simply cannot be understood without this apocalyptic-eschatological dimension. Our differences can also be seen, for example, in the different ways of acknowledging Heidegger. With Rahner it was existential anthropology;

with me it became more and more the question of being and time, or, that is to say, of being as time.

Besides Rahner, were there any other formative figures when you were studying during the fifties?

JBM: I was fascinated by Hans Urs von Balthasar during the early years of my theological studies. I admired his use of language and the way that he crossed the borders between theology, philosophy and literature. Or the way he wrote polemical books. It seems to me that nobody realizes anymore that a totally different Balthasar is hidden behind the later Balthasar. Today I wonder whether it was really more the aesthetic dimension to his theology that I admired than specific contents. I can still remember when his essay, "Theology and Holiness," appeared, toward the end of the fifties. This essay had a tremendous influence on me. Or his *Heart of the World,* and the way he posed christological questions. In his use of language he reminded me of Nietzsche. I had already read Nietzsche in school, secretly during the German classes—and naturally I was greatly impressed.

As far as content goes, Rahner was always the more important figure for me. A clear break came with Balthasar's mystical commentary on the work of Adrienne von Speyr—I simply found it impossible to follow that material, nor did I want to. But we should not forget that in his last works Balthasar anticipated—if you will—one element of postmodernity in the way he conceived of theology as aesthetics. Naturally this has something to do with his diagnostic sense. When it came to specific content, for example in arguments over the Trinity, I always stood decisively in Rahner's camp. Yet it is clear to me that we do an injustice to the multidimensionality of Balthasar's work when we categorize him today simply as the conservative papal theologian. We knew each other well, and our relationship was marked, if I may say so, by mutual respect. We carried on a correspondence—albeit sporadic—even into the eighties.

Let us move on to the philosophical conversation partners with whom you entered into dialogue. How did you, as a young Catholic theologian, happen to come into contact with Bloch and the Frankfurt School?

JBM: As in all decisive moments for me, I first encountered them in conversations and discussion panels—I seldom came across these philosophical figures and positions in books. This has to do with the fact that I have always understood fundamental theology to be one that must risk being defined in terms that are cognitively foreign to it. This is for the sake of its own identity, so that it might become clear about what it really is supposed to be doing: namely, giving an account to others of our hope. Gesturing with a foreign, different *logos,* is a basic passion for me even today.

If you want me to talk about my relationship with Ernst Bloch, then I will have to resort to anecdote. In 1963 I received an invitation from the Academy in Weingarten to a meeting in which Ernst Bloch was participating. The theme was "The Future of Man." At the time I did not have any particularly developed concept of the future, but I had written an essay entitled "The Future of Christianity in a Hominized World." I packed this up and went. The essay really did not have anything to do with Bloch's ideas about the future, but Bloch clearly had the impression that here was a young theologian who talked a bit differently from the other theologians he had met since he had been in the West. At any rate, this is what he once told me. Only after I had become acquainted with him in this way did I begin to read some of his work.

In 1964 there was a broader discussion in Düsseldorf, which many journals reported: a panel discussion between Ernst Bloch and Johann Baptist Metz, a young, unknown theologian from Münster. Bloch was, I think, taken with the way I asked questions, although people were surprised at the way in which Metz "went after" Bloch. When it came to "God" I never gave any ground, but constantly asked him whether Utopia would not fall prey to an anonymous evolution, if there were no God before whom even the past is not fixed. And I have always objected to the way he talked about "transcending without transcendence," responding that one can only do this because there are still some obstinate theologians (like myself) who are talking about "transcendence" as such. His book, *Atheism in Christianity,* ignited passionate discussions on the question of theodicy on a number of Tübingen evenings. In my paperback, *Unterbrechungen,* I used my journals to talk about this, as well as about other meetings with Bloch. We appeared together at a university ceremony in Vienna in 1966, as well as in the Alpbacher College Forum in 1968,[3] and he always defended me when things occasionally got too "pious" for others.

There is less talk about Adorno and Horkheimer in your books than there is about Bloch—although you have a vision of non-identity in common with them. Did you have any discussions and debates with them?

JBM: I became personally acquainted with Adorno in the mid-sixties at a meeting of a student organization, where I spoke as a theologian. Admittedly, at that time I already knew something about Adorno, much more than I had about Bloch. Even today I am amazed at the interest Adorno showed in me. I was fascinated by his eyes, by his intelligence, and above all by his "negative dialectics." I still am today.

That was when I first realized that the thinkers who were having the most influence on me came from a Jewish background. After all, this is also the case with Horkheimer. I was involved with him in a debate in Düsseldorf similar to the one with Bloch. As we were parting at the train station, Horkheimer said to me: "Do you see how cruel a train is, Herr Metz, how it moves off so quickly and separates people from one another?" This was probably meant as a practical critique of the excesses of instrumental reason. I only remember responding, "But after all, Herr Horkheimer, it does not just draw people apart, it also brings them together." Obviously, at the time I was defending the promise of technology, but I don't remember any other details. My involvement with Horkheimer was not all that deep.

In Jürgen Habermas one finds marginal remarks on Metz, and in Metz on Habermas. What are your differences with "critical theory" today?

JBM: My contact with Jürgen Habermas really comes primarily through my students, some of whom are really passionate Habermasians. I became more familiar with Habermas' work for the first time because of my student and friend, Helmut Peukert, in connection with his crucially important dissertation. With all the respect I have for the great significance of his philosophical work, I miss something in Habermas that was very important to me in Benjamin, in Adorno, and even in Horkheimer: the sting of a kind of negative metaphysics. To this day I do not really understand how Habermas can talk about "post-metaphysical thinking," when he himself holds that thinking has so much competence for truth [*Wahrhaftsfähigkeit*]. I suspect that Anglo-

Saxons in particular could shake him more than did the
fathers of the Frankfurt School. Habermas and I are roughly
the same age. Since working together on the Suhrkamp
jubilee volume, since some time together in Boston, since
meeting at the Gießener Philosophical Congress, and since
the Frankfurt debate over "the future of the Enlightenment," we have had more and more personal contacts. We
now see each other more often, not only in public venues,
but also privately.

Great figures in philosophy—think for example of the
later Bloch—are somewhat suspect of ending too close to
the theologians. Not so with Habermas. In this regard there
has been no mutual reception but all kinds of questions and
disagreements. Shall I give you some of the decisive ones,
from my perspective? For example, there is our argument
over what I have called "anamnestic reason"—the argument
over whether and how it is at home in the history of Greek-
inspired thinking, and whether it is not more fundamental
than Habermas' favored candidate: communicative reason.[4]
Analogously, from the perspective of an anamnestic ethics,
I have some reservations about his discourse-ethics and its
scope. For me memories are not just the objects of a testing
discourse, but rather the ground of discourse, without
which they would collapse into a vacuum. They can not only
launch discourse or illustrate it, but also interrupt and halt
it. I know of really only one absolutely universal category: it
is the *memoria passionis*. And I know of only one authority
which cannot be revoked by any Enlightenment or emanci-
pation: the authority of those who suffer. I will risk this con-
jecture here: perhaps what makes Habermas appear less
theological than Benjamin and the early Frankfurt School,
but also in my view always more of an idealist, is the Jewish
background, which is missing or only dimly illuminated in
him. For example, in what is his a priori notion of the ideal
communicative community grounded, on what quasi-idealist

confidence in reconciliation? Is it anything other than an anticipated reconciliation and "sublation" [*Aufhebung*] of the negative? And is this typically German idealism? Here I sense in him too little patience as a thinker with negativity, non-identity, the ban of images and negative theology, if I may put it this way. With his critique of the theological roots of the "Dialectic of Enlightenment" has not Habermas perhaps been too harsh and traded in that position for a disguised idealism? But it would probably be better to put this to him in person and find out first if he has already dealt with this suspicion in some way or another. In any event, meeting him has been a great gift for me.

One of your most recent books is called *Eyes for the Others* *[Augen für die Anderen],* **invoking thereby a philosopher who has received a great deal of attention lately in philosophical discussions: Emmanuel Lévinas. Has Lévinas become more important to your post-idealist theology over the last few years?**

JBM: I met Emmanuel Lévinas for the first and only time in 1985, at Castel Gandolfo. He came up to me and embraced me without saying a word, and I could only interpret this as a sign of his recognition that I have tried with all my might to sharpen Christianity's and theology's conscience about the catastrophe of Auschwitz. That catastrophe certainly stands in the background of Lévinas' philosophy. I will risk saying this much, even though I must confess that I am not very familiar with his writings. Doing some research a while ago I found that I had referred to a French article of Lévinas' as early as 1964, when I was attempting for the first time in my lectures to develop a theological theory of intersubjectivity. But he has never become my teacher, not even during the period when I turned much more deliberately to

Jewish traditions in theological thought. I heard from him, although sporadically, and if I refer to him, it is mainly due to the area of my work. It also is due to the people I am working with and to my many philosophically oriented friends. It is more through them than through Lévinas' primary texts that I have become acquainted with the significance of his so-called "alterity theorem."

Naturally I have been struck by the power of his vision regarding the mystery of the other person in his or her otherness, as well as of how much we have turned the other into a more or less positive or negative function of ourselves, of our questions about our own identity and about becoming selves, all under the pressure of the metaphysical way of thinking-by-assimilation that comes down to us from the Greeks [*griechisch-metaphysischen Angleichungsdenkens*]— and this still happens even in our theories of intersubjectivity. He also sees how little we have grasped the distance and strangeness that separates us from the other, that can never be sublated. He understands how little we have grasped the command in the other's countenance, bidding us to let him or her be the other. I am intrigued by the distinction he suggests between Jewish commentary and Christian hermeneutics; I am intrigued by the way he deals with the semantic contents of the biblical traditions as a whole, particularly to the degree that they contain commandments and imperatives. What, for example, does the commandment to love one's enemy "mean"? When it comes to something like this, can you first get a real sense of what it means in order then to decide whether or not to follow it? Lurking in the background here is a biblical "primacy of praxis," a connection between obedience and understanding which I, at any rate, have not inquired into deeply enough.

Moreover, what I find interesting in Lévinas is the fact that he has also dealt with Heidegger. Like Heidegger, Lévinas has obviously worked through the entire history of

Greek and Western thought, and is trying to show how much it has fallen under totalitarian pressure which derives from an assimilatory mode of thought [*Angleichungsdenken*]; and he also sees that not even Heidegger has been able successfully to overcome this mode of thinking. Of course he has no illusions at all about Heidegger's National Socialist views and his thinly veiled anti-Semitism.

In the early years of your theological work Heidegger was a central concern, and also in connection with Rahner's theology. Yet in the intervening years Heidegger has become virtually taboo in political theology. What do you think about this today?

JBM: My relationship to Heidegger was and still is divided. Don't forget that when I was twenty-two I wrote a philosophical dissertation entitled "Heidegger and the Problem of Metaphysics." At that time I worked through the theme relying on ideas I had been given in the new Thomism: from philosophers like Max Müller, Johannes Lotz, Bernhard Welte, and already, throughout this work, from Karl Rahner's reflections on philosophy and the philosophy of religion, as he had laid them out in his two chief philosophical works (which I later re-edited): *Spirit in World* and *Hearer of the Word.* At the time I really did not notice the issues and problems that theology had gotten itself into with Martin Heidegger's *Being and Time.*

We will come back to this very important question. But first, why the distance, why the lack of understanding for Heidegger?

There are a number of reasons. A political theology that conceives of itself as a theology after Auschwitz would have to be rather disgusted with Heidegger, given his Rector's Address, as well as, after the war, his "Letter on Humanism," in which he simply forgot about the Jews. Yet there were also, to be sure, reasons of a strictly "systematic" nature. On the one hand, it has always been very important to political theology to empower the subject in his or her historical and social conditions, and not in an abstract subjectivity. This would have to make Heidegger's subjectless expressions and his Being devoid of human beings look suspicious. But the most important one, inner-theologically, was this: political theology understood itself from its very beginnings as a critical corrective to the personal, existential, and transcendental theologies that predominated in the fifties and sixties. For Karl Rahner, and by the way for Bultmann as well, Heidegger had an impact above all because of his existential anthropology. Political theology's objection to these theologies based on an existential anthropology was that the price they paid for being compatible with modernity was privatization. Political theology's critique thus turned into a critique of the way Heidegger was being received in theology. Hardly anyone realizes these days how "existential" theological discourse was in the fifties. In its tendency toward existential dramatics this existentialism was, of course, typical of philosophy after the war. Political theology also saw in this sort of existentialism a system of thought which believed that, with people like Heidegger, it had put the Enlightenment behind it, particularly the political Enlightenment with its challenges, without really having gone through it. This too made existentialism problematic to political theology. Given all of this, Heidegger was for me a distant and suspect thinker for a long time.

How then could Heidegger return into your thought?

JBM: At some point it became clear to me that the way to take Heidegger seriously in theology was not through his anthropology, that is, his existential anthropology, but rather through his ontology of time, specifically his program for the temporalization of metaphysics that he was looking for in that ontology. This is connected with the fact that questions concerning apocalypticism have accompanied my theological work from the very beginning, and that later on it was no longer theological anthropology that stood in the foreground of my critical discussions with transcendental theology but theology of history and eschatology. But what the apocalyptic and eschatological really force us to do is to consider questions about the relationship between "God and time." For his ontology of time Heidegger had directed his question back into presocratic thought. To this day I am convinced that he would have done better to look at apocalyptic traditions. For they have the authentic teachings about time. Thus for me, Heidegger really hit upon an epochal theme with *Being and Time*, but he followed it in the wrong direction.

NARRATIVE AND MEMORY—AESTHETICS AND ETHICS

Despite the philosophical impregnation of your theology and despite the confrontations and conversations that you have pressed forward on this level, for some years you have fought vigorously for an entirely different form of language: the recognition of the importance of narrative for humanity, for faith and theology. Why?

JBM: This is an absolutely central and decisive issue. Narrative and narrating are so important—that is, for our human identity and the formation of life—because of what a human being represents, what we ought to hold true about the human, what we can hope for; and we should think about it only in a coalition between those who are alive today and those who have died, been forgotten, sacrificed, or vanquished in the past. Their visions and their wisdom form the basis of humanity, but we can never get access to those resources by means of historical reconstruction alone. We need narration "against time," and that is why we must try again and again to tell stories. Or, to put it differently, a science of history without the aid of literature is formally unavoidable and important, but it can never open up and make available the reserves of wisdom which the *humanum* needs to defend itself.

It is surprising in this regard that you have always expressed skepticism, to the point of rejection, concerning theological attempts to find nourishment in literature. What is your relationship to beauty, to art, music and literature? How can this be compatible with your appreciation for narrative and your own art of speaking and writing?

JBM: Maybe I know a bit better than some of my colleagues that even Christian theology would starve without the bread of narrative. Christianity is at its roots a community of narrative and memory. In becoming theological, it also became a community of argumentation. But in any case the latter always reflects a narrative community. My reservations concerning aesthetics and literature have to do with the fact that these days aesthetics has become an ersatz religion, and history is understood exclusively in a literary fashion, in a postmodern manner, as it were. Yet I try to hone my language, I strive for metaphors into which the entire course of an argument can be gathered up. Still, they are legitimate only insofar as what they say cannot be adequately expressed in any other formulation, the way it is in poetry, for instance. It can even happen that I can start in the morning with three pages of a manuscript, and in the afternoon, after hours of work, a page and a half are left, all for the sake of the idea and the language. Perhaps that is rather old-fashioned of me, but the linguistic power of theology is very important to me. I do not know whether I would call this "aesthetic" or "literary." It's just the way it is. I know that there is a danger in this—if the language takes off, if the radicality of faith ends up being defined as an aesthetic radicality.

Of course, this is where I should also say something about the connection between theological language and the language of prayer. For ultimately all talk about God stems from talking with God. This is what marks out the domain proper to theological language, particularly for a semantically disciplined theology. Here, by the way, I am still following in the footsteps of my teacher, Karl Rahner. At its core, theology can never be adequately separated from mystagogy. But you wanted to hear something about my stance toward beauty, toward art and music. To be honest, I have to be quite prosaic and admit that I have never lost a certain resentment from my childhood. When I was a little boy I had to play the violin, although I would have much rather played soccer. It's different when it comes to language. At any rate, during my student days I had some practice in different areas of language. I have written fairy tales, I have earned some money on the side doing advertising copy, and I even tried my hand at poetry now and then, at an age when my colleagues at the university had long outgrown their own poetic golden age. But what is the point of these private reminiscences? It is important that narrative language not atrophy in our day to day lives.

**Do everyday stories have a theologically relevant moment
which does not have anything explicitly to do with
Christianity? Does our time call for a "narrative culture"?**

JBM: Narrative language is not just for entertainment or
diversion. It can be full of resistance; indeed it may be quite
subversive. In developing a narrativity thesis, I referred in
an earlier work to a film by François Truffaut. I think it was
called *Fahrenheit 451,*[5] and it was about men and women
who, after the brutal destruction of their books and
libraries, had learned their stories by heart, as a wisdom
that resisted oppression and manipulation. This narrative
language is less important today for resisting the destruction of our linguistic worlds by political dictatorships and
totalitarian regimes (although, as we know, they can have a
horrifically destructive impact on language). Today it is
more a matter of saving the language we create and speak
from the gentler dictatorship of our mass media world.
Much damage is done to our language; we are being dis-
possessed of it. I even think it would not be too much to say
that a narrative culture in everyday life would constitute a
culture of resistance.

Such a narrative culture would also be important in view
of what in the Christian world and in theology we call a
"crisis of tradition," a crisis which ultimately does not
endanger just the roots of religion, but the roots of humanity as well. Traditions in which one must become practiced
before reflecting on them are not passed on linguistically
by reflectively rigorous language, not by the language of
the sciences. They are passed on by the primarily narrative
language of the everyday. A culture that does not want to
fall victim to amnesia, that does not want to lose touch
completely with those memories that shape its life, must in
this sense always have something like a narrative culture
within it.

Narrative is in no way a purely privatistic category. This has been misunderstood by many who have asked what narrativity has to do with political theology. Political culture these days is in large measure dependent upon narrative language. Where does the disturbing sense of alienation, indeed the increasing hostility in our multicultural life, originate? One of the reasons is that narrative language has withered among us. The foundational language of intercultural exchange is not technological or scientific language; nor is it the language of politics-as-usual. It is really narrative language. Where it has not itself already been manipulated, the latter is the language of exchanging experiences, the language of wonder, a language free of violence.

Rioting against foreigners and hatred for Jews are again beginning to surface in our midst at the end of the century, and in Europe as a whole: has this taken you by surprise?

JBM: As far as Germany goes this has not surprised me very much. I have never really had much confidence in German normalcy in this regard. More surprising to me is the fact that it is gradually growing into a phenomenon that spans all of Europe. This is certainly something that we must not ignore. Lack of memory certainly has played a role, but obviously there are many other reasons. I must honestly admit that I had not expected the ethnic principle to break into politics once again. The return of nationalism, not just of the nation, was also something that surprised me. On the other hand, I see in what concerns the rebirth of nationalism a chance to clarify our understanding of memory. When I assert that the *memoria passionis* is the only universal category of humanity open to us, I am not thinking of a memory which only serves to affirm us or to secure our identities—rather the opposite: it calls into question our tightly-sealed-up identities. It is a "dangerous" memory; it makes one rather "weak," it creates an open flank. It is a remembrance that does not use suffering to make us aggressive, but reflects on others who suffer. The new nationalisms are all instruments of memory geared toward self-assertion, not of memories that would have us reflect on past suffering.

As far as antisemitism in Germany goes, I am of the opinion that it has to do with the way we carelessly talk about a "new era" and about the definitive end of the post-war period. This is reckless, especially given the political culture of this country. For our painful grappling with our recent past was not simply negative or a sign of weakness, but rather the attainment of a new political culture, one which therefore absolutely must not end up merging into a new "separate German way." These painful dealings with the past could even set a sign of contradiction to the all too robust tendencies toward national and ethnic self-assertions in other parts of Europe.

What I find particularly disturbing lies on a still deeper level. In the history of thought [*Geist*], Jewish spirit [*Geist*], in its very essence, has not found a home in Europe, even though it is clear, for example, how deeply the Ten Commandments are engraved into the ideal of human rights. All of Europe was affected by National Socialism, if for no other reason than that the Jews were to be wiped out all over Europe, that, due to the Nazis, Europe became a "cemetery for the Jews." This reality has not only tragic and moral dimensions; even more, it symbolizes the homeless-ness and vulnerability of the Jewish spirit in Europe. There is something in the Jewish spirit for all of us, above all its gift for anamnesis, about which I have already spoken. It is not only the survival of Christianity and Judaism that is at stake with this anamnestic culture, but rather our very humanity. It is crystal clear that on the day when the computer—which certainly cannot really remember anything, because it cannot forget anything—replaces our capacity for remembrance, we will no longer stage any revolutions against injustices, social or otherwise; for they spring from human beings' remembrance of suffering.

The loss of historical remembrance was also an object of discussion during the historians' debate. The central issue was the so-called "uniqueness" of the mass murder carried out by the National Socialists. How should this be understood? When we talk of the uniqueness of Auschwitz it could not mean that we pay less attention to other suffering. Does not all suffering have its own dignity?

JBM: The way I understand it is that, first and foremost, uniqueness prohibits us from making comparisons. This is a profoundly humane prohibition, because it is based on the dignity of suffering. It is oriented by what I call the authority of those who suffer. When the demands of uniqueness are treated in this way, then the question of whether or not other suffering is tuned out simply does not arise. It is obviously important that this incommensurability be perceived and heeded, whatever the historical context. For me nowhere in the twentieth century does the absolute prohibition against making comparisons—and by such comparisons neutralizing the catastrophe—show itself so clearly and unavoidably as it does in that which we signify with the word "Auschwitz."

Let us move on. Within theology you have been a strong advocate for memory and tradition, and this in a situation in which the standard criticism of the Catholic Church is

that it is too traditional and not "modern" enough. That also divides you from attempts, for example, to connect psychology and theology.

JBM: Let me begin with psychology. I am in no way hostile to psychology. And my critique of the psychologization of our everyday world is a qualified one. It is related to the "ideology," so to speak, of this procedure. It comes to bear when, in a quasi-Nietzschean manner, the project is to transform every metaphysical statement into a psychological one, eliminating transcendence thereby, or when, to be more specific, the God who is not to be adapted to us is eliminated—as if there could only be a God who fits us: either a God who fits our images of self-realization or a God who fits our clerical fantasies. Since the God of whom theologies speak never simply "fits in," theology must always remain critical regarding any attempt to transform everything metaphysical into psychology. Whoever thinks, as a theologian, that psychology and aesthetics give us answers about human beings that are automatically more illuminating or more convincing than those given in the history of religion and of metaphysics simply does not realize that he has sawed off the bough on which he stands. But, to stay with the image, it is not just theology's bough that is sawed off, but anthropology's as well. Wherever everything metaphysical, everything religious, is converted into psychology and aesthetics, it is not just a problem for theology and religion, but also for anthropology and for humanity.

Up until Nietzsche there was still a certain consensus in the critique of religion that went like this: the less religion the more freedom; the weaker the god, the stronger human beings as subjects. Critique of God was presented as the epitome of the Enlightenment. At least Nietzsche uncovered the naiveté of this critique of religion. For him the death of God entailed the death of the human person as well, or, in any case, that human person which we have come to understand heretofore and in modernity's golden age. This is the person presupposed by the Enlightenment, and endowed by the Enlightenment with a capacity for truth and with moral imperatives. Those who dream about overcoming metaphysics with psychology should have no problem at all with this death, once they consult the one who perfected this transformation in his own life's work, that is, Nietzsche. Should theology then end up in a psychopoetically softened Darwinism too?

Now, just a few words on tradition and traditionalism. Traditionalism is to some extent a modern phenomenon. The counter-Enlightenment is a correlate of the Enlightenment; fundamentalism is modernity's stepchild. And why? Because in many respects the Enlightenment has only succeeded halfway, or in the abstract, because modern reason has too little respect for that memory which for its part is the foundation of all critique, including every critique of religion. We have so much traditionalism and so much fundamentalism because we have so much abstract Enlightenment, so much Enlightenment cut in half, so much Enlightenment that has not cultivated memory. Only in and with this cultivated memory could the Enlightenment get beyond itself and enlighten those now-hardened contradictions it carries along with it. Here we should not confuse cause and effect when criticizing thinking that is guided by memory, i.e., anamnestic reason.

Any religious institution deserving the name is formed by traditions. These institutions easily slip over into traditionalist attitudes because tradition as a culture, as an anamnestic culture, can and does operate in a way that is thoroughly critical of institutions as well. Wherever tradition and memory are taken seriously they are always dangerous for the representatives of these traditions too. They are, as I have often said, dangerous memories pointing us toward conversion and transformation. It is precisely—or, to be more realistic, it ought to be precisely—the anamnestic culture within the church that makes it an *ecclesia semper reformanda*. Traditionalism and fundamentalism are by no means unwavering expression of this anamnestic culture, but its contradiction and betrayal.

It is not just Judaism that is constitutively founded in remembrance, but Christianity as well. If memory runs dry, then no Platonism or Idealism will save our Christian identity. Perhaps the most catastrophic heritage of Christian anti-Judaism is that we have lost sight of this. The way we deal with Auschwitz in the church today is a test, a sign, of whether we are nurturing the self-assertion of traditionalism, or more disturbing traditions; whether we celebrate anamnesis only cultically in the Eucharist, or whether we also develop an anamnestic culture in our everyday world.

THE QUESTION OF TIME AND SUFFERING UNTO GOD[6]

Your theological contributions are full of observations that diagnose the times. Besides systematic-theological reasons, are there personal ones?

JBM: I can certainly say that. Something you might call an anticipatory imagination has always played a key role for me. I have always formed for myself images of things which could be grasped only in a shadowy way, in their outlines, things that have not become fully clear to me yet. That can happen with people, with situations, but also with thoughts and ideas. Perhaps this has to do with the way I imagine time, that time proceeds with interruptions, but also with a certain life-pulse and with surprises. This "anticipatory element" is sometimes so strong in me that I wonder if it is partly impatience, partly anxiety over the present, partly unhappy consciousness, partly discontent, and perhaps even the fear of sticking primarily with that which "is." In a controversy with the late Cardinal Höffner someone had defended me to him, saying: "But after all, Metz loves his church." Höffner was supposed to have responded, "Metz loves a church which does not yet exist." Yes, somehow I breathe air that blows from the end time. Despite this, my feet remain on the ground. When I speak about Christendom's capacity for the future, it is not an empty, groundless optimism about the future. For me, the future prospects of Christianity are so weak because so much of its past was squandered. My look toward the future is not simply flight, it is simply irresponsible. As I already said, there are dangerous memories.

With your plea for remembrance, can we not, despite everything, pose this counter-question: Is the church sufficiently "contemporary"? In dealing with tradition, is it not true that instead of "productive non-contemporaneity" that you advocate, there is too much non-productive non-contemporaneity?

JBM: Yes, certainly—and too much backwardness arising out of resentment. With all its non-contemporaneity, the church looks mostly old-fashioned, not at all like an explosive force which exposes and breaks open our banalities, those things that we take to be "modern." What does it really mean after all to be "contemporary"? Who defines this "cutting edge"? For example, am I on the cutting edge of the times, am I up to date, when I live the way commercial television models as a "way of life"? Am I "on the cutting edge" then? I think that there is much that is banal and seamy—a seamy side that is often far below our metaphysical dignity as human persons—in what we like to pass off as being "contemporary," or praise as being in tune with the times.

Of course there are more serious things to be said about "the cutting edge of the times." There is too much going on. There is a great deal of turbulence and excitement over this "cutting edge," one could say a great deal of frenzied and thoughtless excitement, rushing ahead without knowing where we are going. In the words of Samuel Beckett, "Anything and everything goes its way." This is probably the deeper root of all the moroseness, weariness and resentment that we are bemoaning these days, especially in political life, but also in our common life in society as a whole. Those who find our times hard to bear are easily left behind; but perhaps they are the only ones who really know what is going on.

Christianity should not aspire to be the good conscience of a highly mobile, bourgeoisie that has "arrived." By being on the "cutting edge," or "in tune with the times," Christianity could easily become superfluous.

Time and its diagnosis have always been a concern of yours, as are the apocalyptic texts of the Bible. In the mainline churches apocalyptic thought and apocalyptically formed faith have played no essential role—that is a monopoly of sectarianism. Do you think "apocalyptically"? What is the difference between apocalyptic belief and picturing to oneself scenarios for the end of the world?

JBM: I have never supported an apocalypticism that comes up with calculations about time and tries in this sense to get a glimpse at the good Lord's cards. On the other hand, I really think that modern theology has not let itself be provoked enough by the tradition of the apocalyptic sects found throughout all cultures. The basic idea is that any kind of Judaism or Christianity that has lost sight of the end times has already come to an end.

It may be that in becoming accustomed to the smartly presented centuries-old contrast between Judaism and Christianity, we have also lost touch with something of that apocalyptic wisdom passed down in the common biblical traditions. As hard as it is to get across today, the apocalypse in biblical traditions is not a neurotic or inquisitive calculation of the point of time at which the world will end; rather, it is a perception of the world in light of the knowledge of its end. I think that an eschatology developed with apocalyptic intensity is the authentic, culturally understandable dowry of the biblical spirit. This kind of eschatology was unknown in Mediterranean as well as Asian cultures. I make this observation primarily from the perspective of cultural anthropology or the history of cultures. It should lead us to ask whether we have not squandered or cast off too hastily something that is perhaps the decisive dowry of Judaism and Christianity, all because we are anxious to fit easily into the modern age.

Dealing with the end time certainly does not mean resignation. Rather, people become resigned when they assume that there really is no end at all anymore, that is, when they feel that they, and all life, have been sucked into the wake of an anonymous, endless world time, which eventually rolls over each of us like a wave over a grain of sand. The osmotic pressure of evolution on biographical time is growing and swallows up life into its endlessness, if I may put it that way. Our biographical time loses its contours, its final validity, its particularity.

I think that the question of time is a factor in nearly all the intellectual discussions that Christianity is involved in today, even if often a hidden one, and that it is possible to classify the different positions by whether they think in terms of time with a finale, or without. Once again

Nietzsche is relevant in this regard. The Nietzschean image of time as the eternal return of the same is very deeply rooted, and it becomes evident in those forms of escapism—notions of transmigration of souls, reincarnation, and so on—in which people are trying these days to find their identities, identities which indeed they apparently cannot take for granted anymore. I think that it takes a tremendous amount of intellectual courage to press for time with a finale, a notion of time that goes beyond the insight that the individual's life is short. I have encountered an extraordinary degree of interest in this issue in all of my non-theological conversation partners, all of whom, if I were to ask them, would hold themselves to be non-believers in the usual sense. The question always came up: What could you really say to us? Is there something that theology knows that we do not already know or have not over time already given up on? Something that we might call an apocalyptic dowry absolutely belongs among those ideas that the Jewish-Christian traditions can authentically bring to bear here.

Does this mean that if time has no end then religion might very well exist, but no saving God?

JBM: Yes, that is exactly right. As I see it, an important attribute of God, in a way God's eschatological mark, is that God is the end that brings to an end. Of course this also means that when it comes to God there are still things that are yet to be known, even for us Christians. And this goes for Christology too. It must be possible to understand even that as negative theology, especially if we do not want to turn it into an ideology.

From time to time it strikes me that the language of prayer knows more about what is still outstanding, is more deeply formed, so to speak, by negative theology, than the official language of theology itself. Here I am thinking less of the biblical language of prayer, and of the way prayer happens and has happened in the history of religions as a whole. It seems to me that this language of prayer is far more willing to take risks than the logos of theology. The language of prayer is familiar with the painfully enigmatic character of human existence, of how problematic it is in view of God. Elie Wiesel once quoted Kafka, who said that he did not know what theology is, what speech "about" God is, if at all one could only speak "to" God. Here something decisive is said on the origin of God. Theology, then, would really be nothing other than a reflexive language. This might strike many as too pious. But what does that really mean? The language of prayer (prayer, to say it again, looked at as a whole and not just formulaic prayers) is by and large much more dramatic and rebellious than the balanced and measured language of theology when it speaks "about" God. This language of prayer strikes me as being much more unyielding, much more able to resist. It is not ready to fit in, nor is it looking for any consensus or approval among men and women. It often ends in a single cry, or even in nothing but a voiceless sigh of the creature. This language is without barriers. Ultimately, one can say anything to God, even that one cannot believe in God, if only one tries to say it to God. In that sense prayer language contains a great deal of wisdom concerning what I just said: when it comes to God there is always something still open, and even in theology we must have unconditional respect for that.

This is the root of the primacy of eschatology in my theological work, even while I know that as a Christian I am committed to Christology. Christology is certainly not to be shortchanged; it is rather a matter of restoring the inner tensions and drama from its biblical witness.

Not even theology has an answer to every question; it really is not just a game of question and answer. Rightly understood, theological answers are of the sort that the questions and the cry are never forgotten. There are questions for which there are no answers, but theology has a language, a language which turns the questions back toward God. This at any rate is how I understand the so-called theodicy question.

Such a way of understanding theology, this kind of sensitivity to questions, naturally has something to do with my biography; in this regard my life's story and the history of my faith sound together. How could it be otherwise? I admit that throughout my life I have always in some sense felt God's absence. God has never been so clearly present to me as the language of theology tends to insinuate. Now I probably should tell you something from my younger days, something that I briefly wrote about in a festschrift for the bishop of Münster. It is related to an early experience of mine toward the end of the Second World War. I was inducted into the military as a sixteen-year-old student. Together with a company made up of young men more or less my age, I was thrown against the Americans, who, having already crossed the Rhine, were pouring into the country. One night the company commander sent me to battalion headquarters. When I returned the next morning, passing through burning villages and forests, I found nothing but the dead. All I could see were dead faces. To this very day, all I can remember is a soundless cry. I suspect that all my childhood dreams, as well as what people call "childlike trust," disintegrated in that soundless cry.

Subsequently I did not take this experience and this memory to the psychologist but into the church, not to let myself be talked out of this experience and this memory but in order to believe in God and talk about God. Is it any surprise then that my first small book—it is called *The Advent of*

God and came out in 1959—already invoked apocalyptic imagery? Is it any surprise that a hint of uneasiness and of something unreconciled is discernible in my theological language if I talk about feeling God's absence? I think that there are many, many people who have experiences just like mine and who talk about them using this sort of language, or even none at all. I would like to do theology for them too, particularly for them: for people who have no intact, undamaged images of hope, for those whose childhood dreams have fallen apart. It is very important to me not to treat these questions on the margins, or apologetically, in the antechamber to "real" theology, but rather to give voice to them in the center of our talk about God. Life has taught other theologians not, certainly, to believe something different, but to believe differently. They will in turn do theology differently.

How can Christology still be formulated under these premises? Does a negative Christology follow from a negative theology?

JBM: Let me answer tentatively: In my opinion what we need in Christian theology is an element of what I have called for some time a Holy Saturday Christology.[7] If I can put it this way, in Christology we have lost the way between Good Friday and Easter Sunday. We have too much pure Easter Sunday Christology. I feel that the atmosphere of Holy Saturday has to be narrated within Christology itself. For a long time now not everybody has experienced Easter Sunday as the third day after Good Friday. The experience of the resurrection is a highly non-contemporaneous event. We all know how Paul portrays it in 1 Corinthians. First we have the women who, according to Mark, are frightened and speechless; then Peter and John; much later the disci-

ples on the road to Emmaus; at another time Thomas; later
still the larger number of disciples in the scene by the sea;
much, much later Saul on the road to Damascus, and so on.
What I want to say is this: The story of a journey is integral
to Christology. What is called for is the experience of Holy
Saturday and precisely the kind of Holy Saturday language
in our Christology which is not, as in mythology, simply the
language of the victor.

In theology, the eschatological statements that are integral
to Christology are for the most part removed and shifted over
into the doctrine of the last things. For example, there is the
so-called doctrine of the second coming, which in this ter-
minology is very much open to misunderstanding, but cannot simply be dispensed with altogether. The doctrine of
the second coming is a statement about the Son of Man and
about the Christ. Consequently, it belongs to the very center of Christology itself. What this shows is that theology is
tempted to remove from Christology everything that still
might irritate us temporally—what I previously called the
journey element. Theology is tempted to pass over in
silence what is unsaid about the Son of God.

As I see it there is yet another danger here, which tends
in the same direction. The older Christianity gets, the more
"affirmative" it seems to become, the less negative theology
it seems to tolerate, the more it tries to save itself from the
times by "closing itself off." For me this is one of the reasons why eschatology and apocalypticism have faded out of
our Christology. The lightning bolt of danger appears to be
a thing of the past; the storm is moving off; the thunder
only echoes; darkness and clouds are behind us. Our sense
of the misfortune of others is atrophying; we quickly pass
from the fastness of faith to a fastness of bewilderment, and
anyone talking about vulnerability only appears to be giving
voice to doubt and despair. It seems to me that a pressing
task for theology is to draw our attention to all of this, and

more. If I may say it in such a cursory manner, that way of looking at Christianity's situation is for me personally connected with my belated horror over Auschwitz.

Then in which God can we still believe—especially if we take seriously the fact that we live "after Auschwitz"? In a loving Father? In a redeemer God? In a suffering God?

JBM: Many theologians today talk about the suffering God. I listen respectfully, especially when I reflect on formulations of someone like Dietrich Bonhoeffer, but also expressions of my theologian friends and fellow travelers, like Jürgen Moltmann and Dorothee Sölle. But I myself hesitate with this talk about a suffering God; indeed, I have expressed myself critically on a number of occasions. Here I can only be very brief and say this: Today the talk about a suffering God is intended as a critical rejection of the almighty creator God. One no longer risks speaking of God's omnipotence, given the situation of his creation that cries out to heaven. Were God all-powerful, how else could one think of him except as an apathetic idol or Moloch?

However, those who talk about a suffering and co-suffering God nonetheless presume a particular form of omnipotence, namely, the omnipotence and invincibility of God's love. For how could God be God, and continue to be God, how would God be anything other than the hopeless duplication of our own suffering and our own love, if God's love could itself founder in this suffering and co-suffering? In this case is there not something like a semantic sleight-of-hand going on, if (consciously or unconsciously) we talk about a suffering of God that can never really break down, can never collapse? I have my doubts here.

Is it only a coincidence that there is so much talk in theology, in an almost euphoric tone, about a God who suffers and suffers with us, precisely at a time when aesthetics and aestheticization have taken on a key role in our intellectual culture? To put the question differently: Is there not something like an aestheticization of all suffering that shines through this talk about a suffering God? Suffering is a negative mystery, a mystery of human beings that is untransferrable. I wonder if we are not underestimating the negativity of suffering? After all, at its roots suffering is anything but a powerful or even triumphant and solidaristic co-suffering. It is not even simply a sign and expression of love; rather, it is much more a horrifying sign that one is no longer able to love. Suffering leads into a void unless it be suffering unto God.[8] That is how I see it, and that is one of the reasons why I hesitate when speaking of a suffering God.

Now when it comes to talking about God's omnipotence, we should never forget that every divine attribute also carries an eschatological stamp. The image of a creator God at rest, looking down, as it were, from on high on his suffering creation, is an absolutely incoherent idea which can only lead to cynicism and apathy. However, as I just said, every divine predicate, every ontological statement concerning God, up to and including the Johannine proposition that "God is love," carries a temporal stamp. That forces theologians to use the form of negative theology even when talking about the power of God as creator. Not even creation is something that is simply back there "behind us."

I often use the phrase "God passion."[9] I understand it as an objective genitive, that is, as a passion for God and a suffering unto God, but not in the sense of a subjective genitive, that is, not as suffering *of* God. Here I always insist on a negative theology, and my conviction concerning negative theology is that it is certainly not just a figment of the theologians' intellectual imagination. In my opinion it is the most widespread way of talking about God, particularly if we take the language of prayer into account—and this means not the formulaic, but the spontaneous language of prayer, not excepting the most profound and radical mysticism.

You also asked about the redeemer God. Obviously the idea of redemption is central to Christianity; far be it from me to dispute it. Nonetheless, I would not keep silent over an issue that has occupied me more and more intensively over the past few years. I call this issue—certainly not without risking being misunderstood—the danger of "falling under a soteriological spell." I use such a drastic formulation because I am under the impression that this danger is deeply rooted in Christian theology; indeed, I suspect that it is connected to the wider process through which Christianity became theological. Why? Because I suspect that from its start Christian theology tried to soften or silence a question that accompanies the whole span of biblical traditions: the question of justice for those who suffer innocently. That was done by transforming this question about justice for innocent sufferers into the question about redemption for the guilty. To put it differently, soteriology was supposed simply to replace theodicy or make it superfluous. This too, I have already discussed in great detail, above all concerning the role of Augustine in this process. Of course I cannot repeat all of this to you here. However I would like to point out one consequence which is a part of this process and which accordingly has had an impact on Christianity.

A religion originally sensitive to suffering became a religion emphatically sensitive to sin—indeed, I might say hypersensitive to sin. I have occasionally called this overuse of the idea of sin the Christian absolutism of sin, by which Christian morality focused on suffering is transformed into one exclusively oriented to sin. This has had serious consequences in our time. Human self-understanding and interpretation of freedom has become more and more cut loose from the idea of guilt. A person's capacity for guilt, which in the biblical traditions is virtually *the* mark of human freedom, now has become the antipode to the concept of freedom.

Here lies an important task hardly even broached by Christian theology. How can we better understand the doctrine of original sin in this context? And above all, what about the so-called theodicy question? Has it simply been put to rest by the Christian doctrine of redemption? For me these are questions toward God, for which I certainly have a language but no answer. Integral to these questions (and this is probably the first and essential theodicy question), why does sin exist? why guilt? I learned from Karl Rahner that the usual scholastic answer ("God has to allow sin in order for there to be freedom") is not a convincing one. Obviously for Christian faith there is something like creaturely freedom without sin. Why then, O God, the sinful, guilty creature? Guardini is supposed to have asked this question as he was dying. I have made it my own—as a prayer.

Notes

1. ["Folk church" renders *Volkskirche*, which for Metz indicates the older way of organizing the church in Europe, centered on the village and its religious life, in which secularization processes have not yet been felt. By "bourgeois church" he means a way of organizing the church and the faith in response to those processes; it is (in Metz's view) understood and structured primarily as a service-providing church for middle class individuals.—*trans.*]

2. [Metz is probably alluding to the *Kirchensteur,* a tax collected by the state on behalf of the churches in Germany. By

officially declaring that one is leaving the church (Roman Catholic or Protestant) one can avoid this tax.—*trans.*]

3. [*Alpbacher Hochschulwochen.* This is an international forum sponsored by the Austrian College during the last two weeks of August. The college picks a topic related to science and culture and invites a distinguished panel of experts to speak on it and debate it.—*trans.*]

4. For the concept of "anamnestic reason," and Metz's critique of Habermas, see "Anamnestic Reason: A Theologian's Remarks on the Crisis in the *Geisteswissenschaften,*" in *Cultural-Political Interventions in The Unfinished Project of Enlightenment,* ed. Thomas McCarthy, Axel Honneth, et al. (Cambridge, Massachusetts: MIT Press, 1992).

5. [The film is based on the novel by Ray Bradbury, *Fahrenheit 451* (New York: Simon & Schuster, 1993).—*trans.*]

6. [Suffering unto God translates *leiden an Gott.* A literal translation would be "suffering *from* God," in the sense of suffering from a cold. I have chosen this somewhat idiosyncratic translation to bring out the more dynamic nature of this "state." It is related to another of Metz's favorite phrases: *Rückfragen an Gott,* which means to question God, to come back to God full of questions. Job exemplifies both phrases, as the one who does not just passively suffer "from," but brings his suffering before God, continues to relate to God, albeit angrily and full of questions, from *out of* his suffering.—*trans.*]

7. [It should be noted that "Holy Saturday" (*Karsamstag*) is more strongly tied etymologically to "Good Friday" (*Karfreitag*) in German than it is in English—*trans.*]

8. See note 6 above.

9. [This translates *Gottespassion,* which can be translated either as "passion for God" or "God's passion." Metz reflects on this ambiguity in the following sentences. It is normally translated here in the way that Metz indicates, as "passion for God."—*trans.*]

SUGGESTED READINGS BY JOHANN BAPTIST METZ*

"Gott vor uns: Statt eines theologischen Arguments." In *Ernst Bloch zu ehren*, ed. Siegfried Unseld. Frankfurt: Suhrkamp, 1965, 227–41. *On the concept of the future.*

Zur Theologie der Welt. Mainz: Matthias-Grünewald Verlag, 1968. Translated by William Glen-Doepel as *Theology of the World*. New York: Herder, 1969. *This book deals with the theological significance of secularization and contains the first writings on political theology.*

"Kirchliche Autorität im Anspruch der Freiheitsgeschichte." In *Kirche im Prozeß der Aufklärung*, ed. J. B. Metz, Jürgen Moltmann and Willi Oelmüller. Munich: Kaiser Verlag, 1970. Translated by David Kelly and Henry Vander Goot, as "Prophetic Authority." In *Religion and Political Society,* translated and edited by the Institute of Christian Thought. New York: Harper Forum Books, 1974. *The first outline of a political ecclesiology.*

"Unsere Hoffnung: Ein Bekenntnis zum Glauben in dieser Zeit. Beschluß der Gemeinsamen Synode der Bistümer in der Bundesrepublik Deutschland," Bonn, 1975. *This is a presentation written by J. B. Metz. The German bishops' final decree was changed and expanded, based on discussions during the Synod. This is still today a characteristic and crucial text for Metz's theology.*

Zeit der Orden? Zur Mystik und Politik der Nachfolge. Freiburg: Herder, 1977. Translated by Thomas Linton as *Followers*

---

* (The German originals are given, along with English translations, where available. The annotations [given in italics] are the work of the interviewers. —*trans.*)

of Christ: The Religious Life and the Church. New York: Paulist Press, 1978. *This book deals with the spiritual and theological significance of discipleship, outside the boundaries of religious life, for being a Christian today.*

Glaube in Geschichte und Gesellschaft: Studien zu einer praktischen Fundamentaltheologie. Mainz: Matthias-Grünewald, 1977. Translated by David Smith as *Faith in History and Society: Toward a Practical Fundamental Theology.* New York: Seabury, 1980. *Metz's chief systematic work, this book clarifies the basic concepts and specific positions of his theology.*

Jenseits bürgerliche Religion: Reden über die Zukunft des Christentums. Mainz/Munich: Kaiser-Grünewald, 1980. Translated by Peter Mann as *The Emergent Church: The Future of Christianity in a Postbourgeois World.* New York: Crossroad, 1987. *This work discusses theology after Auschwitz, bourgeois religion, and base Christian communities.*

Unterbrechungen: Theologisch-politisch Perspektiven und Profile. Gütersloh: Gütersloher Verlagshaus, 1981. *This book contains theses on apocalypticism, portraits and other contributions.*

"Unterwegs zu einer nachidealistischen Theologie." In *Entwürfe der Theologie,* ed. Johannes B. Bauer. Cologne: Styria, 1985. Translated by J. Matthew Ashley as "On the Way to a Post-Idealist Theology," in *A Passion for God: The Mystical-Political Dimension of Christianity,* translated and edited, with an introduction by J. Matthew Ashley. Mahwah, N.J.: Paulist Press, 1997, pp. 30–53. *A good, readable introduction to the intentions of Metz's theology and the options it makes.*

"Thesen zum theologischen Ort der Befreiungstheologie," introduction to *Die Theologie der Befreiung: Hoffnung oder Gefahr für dieKirche?* Edited by J. B. Metz. Düsseldorf:

Patmos, 1986. *This essay deals with the controversies surrounding Latin American liberation theology.*

With Franz-Xavier Kaufmann, *Zukunftsfähigkeit: Suchbewegegungen im Christentum.* Freiburg: Herder, 1987. *Metz discusses the "polycentric world church," as well as the talk about the "death of the subject."*

"Theologie versus Polymythie oder: Kleine Apologie des biblischen Monotheismus." In *Einheit und Vielheit: XIV deutscher Kongreß für Philosophie,* ed. Odo Marquard. Hamburg: Felix Meiner Verlag, 1990. Translated by J. Matthew Ashley as "Theology versus Polymythicism: A Short Apology for Biblical Modernism," in *A Passion for God,* 72–91. *This essays deals with "postmodern" thought and the meaning of biblical and historical faith.*

With Hans-Eckehard Bahr: *Augen für die Anderen. Lateinamerika–eine theologische Erfahrung.* Munich: Kindler, 1991. *Metz gives an account of a journey and reflects on the "church of the poor."*

With Tiemo Rainer Peters: *Gottespassion: Zur Ordensexistenz heute.* Freiburg: Herder, 1991. Metz's contribution to this volume is translated by J. Matthew Ashley as "A Passion for God: The Challenge and Promise of Religious Life," in *A Passion for God,* 150–74. *Affirming religion, denying God–Christian existence today.*

"Theologie als Theodizee?" In *Theodizee–Gott vor Gericht?* ed. Willi Oelmüller. Munich: Wilhelm Fink, 1990, 103–118. Translated by J. Matthew Ashley as "Theology as Theodicy?" in *A Passion for God,* 55–71. *An essay that considers suffering, suffering unto God, and the question of the end of time.*

Elie Wiesel

ELIE WIESEL
BIOGRAPHICAL NOTES

Since leaving Sighet, Elie Wiesel writes, he has done nothing but tell stories about it, the town that gave him everything and took it all away. This "tiny, dusty town, somewhere in a far corner of Transylvania, in the shadow of the Carpathians," was home to ten thousand Jews, an eastern Jewish Shtetl strongly influenced by Hassidism, before it was wiped out root and branch. The Hassidic movement, which spread among eastern European Jewry like a raging forest fire and gave hope once again to its persecuted, tormented Jews, had also made its mark on Sighet. Wiesel, born in 1928, whose parents, Shlomo and Sarah, ran a small grocery store, lived entirely in the world of books, stories and prayers that was brought forth by that "religious humanism." His grandfather, Dodye Feig, told him the stories of the old masters over and over again. The first teachers he found were Talmudists and Jewish mystics, who introduced him to the riches of the tradition and the mysteries of Kabbalah.

One morning, just as the young man was putting on his prayer shawl to say the traditional morning prayers, shouting was heard in the street: "Jews out! Get out of your houses!" The expulsion of the Jews had begun. Only late in the summer of 1944, with the help of the local police, did the Nazis begin to carry out their "final solution" in Sighet. The town's Jews were trapped. Transported in sealed boxcars to a small train station—the end of the line—on the other side of the Carpathians, those who stood at the barred windows could make out the name of the place: "Auschwitz." In his autobiographical account of the camps Wiesel writes that no one had ever heard that name before.

He was forever separated from his mother and little sister, Tsipora, in the selection process. Together with his father he had to live through the "kingdom of night," in which they were robbed of all human dignity. After his father had died of sickness, weakness and ill-treatment in Buchenwald—the concentration camp to which the last of Auschwitz's prisoners were taken toward the end of the war—the sixteen-year-old was liberated by American troops in April of 1945. He was taken to France and soon began studying philosophy, psychology and literature in Paris. "I wanted to grasp the meaning of the events of which I had become a victim," are the words he later put in the mouth of one of his characters, who, like all the main characters in his narratives, is a survivor of the annihilation of the Jews. At the same time Wiesel resumed his study of the Hebrew scriptures, guided by a mysterious Talmud teacher.

Everything had changed, however. His naive access to God was closed to him; his faith in human beings was shattered. Barely able to form relationships, he lived distantly, plagued by memories. He increasingly made his living in journalism, which eventually made it possible for him to travel extensively. For ten years he was unable to speak about his experiences. Not a word about Auschwitz. After ten years he passed through the door of silence into literature.

Wiesel's writings are profoundly influenced by Jewish tradition. To this very day everything he writes, he writes as a Jew. His first and most important book, *Night,* is an account of what he lived through in the realm of barbed wire, "that damned, inhuman realm where death was mass-produced the way other factories made toothpaste." This book became the cornerstone of his subsequent creations. Elie Wiesel's work and subsequent biography cannot be understood apart from this all-pervasive experience. The influences of French existentialism and humanism, the impact of reading Franz Kafka, the recourse to biblical,

Talmudic, Kabbalistic and Hassidic motifs: all of these had their effect only as filtered through the abyss of the Shoah, the mass-murder of the Jews under National Socialism.

The question of God undergoes a remarkable intensification as well: in Wiesel's work it is always a question to God: Where were you when your children needed you most? How could you let human beings so befoul your creation? Into his Job-like struggle with God, the survivor takes the cries of the victims, uttered beneath a silent heaven, in the presence of men and women "who are in the likeness of God only in cruelty."

And yet.... One of the most important phrases in Wiesel's work is "And yet." Despite the despair from that event, in that despair, he finds a source of trust in God and in human beings which lies not in forgetting the horror, but precisely in remembering it. Those who died in the furnaces did not find a cemetery; their bodies were transformed into plumes of smoke. The only place that is truly theirs is the remembrance of those who survived and those born after them. If these forget, then they kill a second time. Remembering the victims, human beings have—perhaps—the power to create the present and future in a more human way than in the past.

Memory is the leitmotif both of his fiction and of his essays, his dramas and his writings about Jewish masters and legends. It permeates his commitment to human rights all over the world. In recognition of this he received the Nobel Peace Prize in 1986. The Nobel Committee explained its choice with these words: "Elie Wiesel is one of the most important spiritual leaders and trailblazers of our time. His words proclaim the message of peace, reconciliation, and human dignity."

Yet this message is also conscious of the danger that hovers over it: humanity's memory can wane; the memory of past suffering can be lost. Wiesel's most recent novel, the last of ten to date, breaks off suddenly in mid-narrative. At the end is a half-finished sentence, with no period. The story of someone who forgets, a survivor of Auschwitz who is haunted by the disease of forgetting, remains incomplete. The burning question which dominates the book and guides all of Elie Wiesel's work is this: What happens when the witnesses are no longer able to pass on their message, and their words pass unheeded?

TO BE A JEW—HOPE FROM REMEMBRANCE

At the conclusion of the original version of your first book, *Night*, which has come out in Yiddish with the title, *Un di Welt hot geschwign*, you write that after your liberation from the concentration camp at Buchenwald you smashed a mirror to ward off the vision and power of death and belong once again to the land of the living. Was smashing the mirror worth it?

EW: I asked myself this question even then, and today the answer is yes. However, the question still remains. Every time I look in a mirror I have to ask myself this question. When I look around the world I see nothing but hopelessness. And yet I must, we all must, try to find a source for hope. We must believe in human beings, in spite of human beings.

You know that I am a Jew through and through. My life and my dreams are Jewish. Therefore my sources are the biblical writings, the Torah, Job, the Prophets, yet also the writings of the rabbinic masters, the Talmud, and so on. Since I am a child of Hassidism I draw from Jewish mysticism as well. For me mysticism means searching for the inner reality of reality. Mysticism reveals the existence of a reality other than the superficial, a deeper, eternal reality.

Hassidism wants to bring men and women closer together in order to lead them closer to God. Like Jewish mysticism, it is a movement in search of redemption, striving for redemption, and this means a collective redemption. In other religions and their mystical branches, in Sufism for example, Islamic mysticism, what is at issue is personal, individual salvation. In the Jewish tradition, on the other hand, it is always a matter of the community.

63

**Is it primarily the Jewish tradition that has influenced you
or do you have roots in humanism as well?**

EW: I do not draw my energy just from written sources;
energy derives from human behavior. Consequently it
comes from our fellow men and women, above all from children. When I observe children I am extremely sensitive.
Children can make me despair. Or they can drive out my
despair. When I see children suffer, I feel that I must do
everything in the world to end their suffering, and I would
do it. Then I discover in myself a power that I never knew
existed before; it comes from the children. From all children in general, not just Jewish children. Naturally from
Jewish children too, for I am a Jew. They can be children
from all over, from every nation on earth. When I saw the
children of Biafra, the starving children, I was moved to
tears and to action. When I saw the children of Ethiopia I
was moved to actions and to tears.

It is always the children. Children are the key to my work
and the key to my life. I will never, never accept it when this
world's children are subject to hunger, persecution and
humiliation. From the very beginning, four thousand years
ago in Egypt, Jewish children were continually threatened.
The children were the first whom Pharaoh wanted drowned
in the sea. And ever since those days, whenever Jews are
threatened, it is always the children who are threatened first,
everywhere. When I think about this threat, I naturally think
about the concentration camps too: we have lost more than
a million children. This is something that I will never
understand: how can the world continue to torment its children? This is beyond me. And therefore, whenever I see a
child today, I do not see that child alone, but rather I see
him or her surrounded by those other children who have
disappeared.

For this reason, when it comes to what is most fundamental to me being a Jew and being a human being are one and the same. The Jew in me is a human being, and the human being in me is a Jew. I will say the same thing to you that I say to many young people: I do not believe in racial, ethnic or religious superiority. Not for a moment do I think that my religion is superior to the Christian religion. I do not believe that there is one people on the earth which is superior to the others. I was born a Jew. Therefore Judaism, the Jewish traditions, are my life. It is by being a Jew that I can be human. I would expect that you could say the same thing about your relationship to your religion. But in all of this the key word is tolerance. I would want to be as open as possible to Islam, to Christianity, or to any conviction held by any person whatsoever. I seriously hope that I am open. I would wish that every person would treat me the same.

Is there a chance that the religions of the world can live together in peace, or, to be more concrete, Judaism and Catholicism?

EW: The second question is the simpler one. Since I come from a very religious background I study the history of religions and the philosophy of religions. When I was very young I did nothing but study the Talmud and the Bible. When I took up my lessons I forgot about everything else. That is why I still study today, and I have studied Catholicism too. There have been periods in Catholic history that involved my people which were not particularly happy ones for them. The Inquisition in Spain: I cannot understand it; to this very day I cannot understand it. Recall Dostoevsky; he has a powerful section on the Grand Inquisitor. The Grand Inquisitor, who thinks that everything he does is for Christ. Finally, Christ comes to him, yet he drives him away and says: "You are bothering me. Go away!" I cannot understand how people can be persecuted and put to the torch in the name of love and in the name of love of God. I simply cannot understand it.

Just as little do I understand the Crusades. At the origins of the Crusades there is perhaps a good idea, from a Catholic perspective: to go to Jerusalem and save the holy places. But on the way they killed Jews. Every time. They had nothing to do with Jews, but they killed Jews. I cannot understand it.

I would like to tell you something more, which might be painful for you. I owe it to you to be honest. As a Jew I feel what my people feel. I try to go beyond it and feel what you feel. But the best example is that of the cross. For you the cross is a symbol of love and compassion. Not for my people. For there have been times—naturally not today, but there have been times—when the cross symbolized, indeed incarnated, suffering and horror. Does this mean that Christians today are responsible for that? God forbid! What happened years and centuries ago in Catholic history is not your work. That is why I can come into an open dialogue with you.

Turning to the first part of your question, about the community of religions, I wish I could be more optimistic. I believe that the Messiah will come one day, and then all peoples will joyfully embrace all other peoples. But until then? Until then there are so many problems: religious, economic, political and ecological. Show me a human being who does not have any problems. There aren't any. On the other hand, I do believe that there is progress. Economic progress is taking place all around the globe. More and more Jews and Catholics are meeting one another. More and more Jews and Christians are meeting one another. And Muslims. This is extremely important. We should come together and discuss our past and our present—without any prejudice, without any despair. Just the fact that we can meet with one another is a sign of the greatest, immeasurable hope.

Look. Superficially there are so many things that divide us: you, a young German Christian, and me. Not just age and language, but history. I belong to a people which has experienced tremendous suffering at the hands of your people. I remember this, and you should remember it just as much. This does not mean, this should not mean, that we cannot form a deeply felt relationship. I do not believe—I will repeat this to my dying day—I do not believe in collective guilt. I have never believed in it, and I will never believe in it. I will never accept the idea of collective guilt. Only the guilty are guilty. Only the passive onlookers have some part in this guilt—on a different level. You have struggled with the same question as I: What do we make of our past? I am certain of this: for you it is a burden. For me, no. My past means something different for me. I bear it. I take it up. I want it to become more and more a part of my awareness as well as my consciousness. If possible, I want it to be transformed for me as a writer into an act of creativity. If I were a musician, I would say: into music. One thing is clear to me: I must take hold of yesterday's images and transform them into a bridge, into a connection, a burning connection. And this connection should not separate me from you—rather, the opposite. It should bring me closer to you and, so I hope, also you to me.

You talk about remembrance of the events of the past. What place does it take in your work?

EW: I have written many books; perhaps some would say too many. I have written about the Bible and about the Talmud. I have written about Hassidism and Jerusalem. I have written on so many different themes that one morning a few years ago I suddenly began to wonder what all my books have in common. They tell of such diverse times and so many different themes, subjects which are so different from one another. What do they have in common? Their commonality is the obligation to remember. When I talk about the Akedah, the biblical binding of Isaac, or when I recount the story of the founder of Hassidism, the Besht, the master of holiness, of the Good Name, or when I tell stories about Jerusalem or—rarely—about our tragedy, it is the obligation to remember that drives me to take pen in hand and write one word after another. I ask myself what the opposite of memory is. The opposite of memory is the sickness of forgetting, what today we call Alzheimer's Disease. That is why I wrote a novel about it. I must tell you that it is one of the saddest stories I have written yet. I thoroughly studied this disease. I have met with its victims and with their families. There is no escape from it. Anger can be creative. Anger can represent the beginning of growth. Alzheimer's, or forgetting, is the end.

For these reasons my message is a very simple one: Never fight against memory. Even if it is painful, it will help you; it will give you something; it will enrich you. Ultimately, what would culture be without memory? What would philosophy be without memory? What would be love for a friend without remembering that love the next day? One cannot live without it. One cannot exist without remembrance.

LITERARY AND RELIGIOUS TEACHERS

Language is for you the medium of memory. Who was your literary teacher?

EW: I do not have a single teacher for the way I write. It is the sum, the totality of many works which have influenced me: biblical writings because of the density of their prose

and the way they concentrate on particular ideas. Greek
and Latin works of antiquity as much as the Talmud and the
stories of the Hassidic masters have influenced me. I have
also learned much from modern literature, a little bit from
every author. When I read Kafka he is the most important
influence on my writing; when I read Dostoevsky or
Thomas Mann it is he.

However, the Jew Kafka has been particularly formative
for me. I remember how I discovered Kafka. I was a student
in Paris in 1946. An acquaintance gave me one of Kafka's
books, the first one I read. It was *The Trial.* I began reading
in the afternoon and read the whole night through. Usually
in Paris, the garbage collectors come around six in the
morning and make a frightful racket. Every day I would get
enraged at it, and not just at it, but at the whole world. But
that morning, what I most wanted to do when the din
forced its way into my room was to run down, throw open
the door, rush out into the street and embrace the garbage
collectors, just for reminding me that another world besides
Kafka's still existed out there. I hold Kafka to be one of the
greatest writers of our time. He has divided the history of
literature into before Kafka and after Kafka.

**In your novel, *Abenddämmerung in der Ferne,* there are
many allusions to Kafka's writings. Is there a connection
between the mountain clinic that is the center of the plot,
and Kafka's "castle"?**

EW: No, surely not. Perhaps an unconscious one—who
knows? Some commentators make a connection with
Thomas Mann's *Magic Mountain,* but this is not valid either
on a conscious level. This novel is influenced by both Kafka
and Thomas Mann, so it is possible that *The Castle* is inte-
grated into it in some way or another. However, with Kafka

we don't know what happens in the "castle." In my novel one does not know what is happening outside the clinic, the lunatic asylum. In *The Castle* Kafka reaches into the depth of despair, the innermost heart of absurdity. Kafka's problem was absurdity. I do not think that this is my issue. Mine is injustice. I am not concerned with the absurdity of human existence but rather with the injustice of human existence. Frequently absurdity is unjust, but not every injustice is absurd.

Camus has also had an influence on you, and his work takes up the absurd and injustice at the same time.

EW: Yes, I have taken a great deal from Camus, particularly his focus on social problems and his commitment to humanity. What grips me deeply, however, is this: a while ago the last of Camus' journals appeared in France. During the last six years of his life he was unspeakably sad. He fell into despair, almost chronic depression. Why was he, who embodied the best and most pure of what we call a humanist, so much in despair at the end of his life?

Besides humanism there is, as you said, the Jewish influence. Somewhere you wrote that in post-war Paris you had the same Talmud teacher as Emmanuel Lévinas.

EW: That is correct. Lévinas and I knew each other well; we were very close. For years we had the same teacher, Harav Shoushanie, but we did not take lessons together. We did not know each other at that time. I was his student and still very young. Lévinas, who was older than I, was also his pupil, the student of a great, but disturbed, master. The difference between Lévinas and me is that Lévinas is no Kabbalist; he is a rationalist. I myself am a student of

Kabbalah, Jewish mysticism. I would not say that I am a Kabbalist, but just a student of Kabbalah. I love the Kabbalah. I love it for its beauty and find in it a great deal of beauty and truth. Kabbalah is a creative way to discover life, not only as it is, but as it could look in the imagination of the mystic. The Kabbalist is not wrapped up in history; on the contrary, he wants to overcome history. Gershom Scholem has shown that Kabbalah means either to understand the mystery of the beginning, or to bring about the end of history, the messiah. No rationalist thinks this way. In Kabbalah there is the idea of "leaping"—one can jump right out of a rational investigation. That is the difference from Talmud. Talmud is rational, Kabbalah is not. In Talmud we are always coming across the command, "Come and hear." In Kabbalah it is "Come and see." There we find vertical thinking, in contrast to horizontal thinking.

Looking at my own work, I can say that I owe much more to Kabbalah than to rationalism, since I am convinced that what happened in Auschwitz is a result of rationalism. The deep significance of that event, the Shoah, transcends reason. Knowing the past, we can grasp today how it happened. It was an interruption of history, which does not mean that it lies outside history. Auschwitz did not fall from heaven. Read, for example, Luther's statements about the Jews, or think back on other historical testimonies.

There are many parallels between you and Lévinas. Have you been influenced by him?

EW: No, influence is the wrong word. Nor did Martin Buber influence me, and yet there are parallels. We draw from similar sources, the sources of Judaism, and each of us understands them in his own way. As a result there are naturally some commonalities. As I already said, Lévinas and I were very close and we used to see each other now and then in Paris; we should have met much more often. However, his roots are not in the Hassidic tradition, but rather in an anti-Kabbalist movement of east-European Judaism, that is, Lithuanian rationalism. There do appear to be Kabbalistic motifs in Lévinas' work, and as a Jewish thinker he cannot wholly escape the influence and aura of Kabbalah. But those motifs also surface with other currents of Judaism; in Jewish philosophy, for instance, they show up in Maimonides. Maimonides was no Kabbalist. I do think that he was, nevertheless, a mystic, but I am probably the only one with this conviction.

You often invoke Jewish mysticism, Kabbalah. After Auschwitz can we go back to it in an unbroken way?

EW: I am not sure whether or not there is a connection between Kabbalah and Auschwitz. The only connection might be a mystical one. Auschwitz can only be the absolute revelation of something absolute, of absolute evil. Occasionally I have made a connection between Auschwitz and the revelation on Sinai, where the Torah was handed down. Auschwitz had an immense impact: it changed humanity, history, our perception of human beings, the meaning of certain words that we can no longer use. It has had a tremendous effect on the recognition of limits and the absence of limits in regard to persons, be they good or evil. All of this is Kabbalah. The Kabbalah talks about limitlessness, and here we have something without limits. With horror we find out that there is not only something limitless when it comes to good, but also regarding evil. Thus, the two are very close, and I believe there is a connection between Kabbalah and Auschwitz. This does not mean that I can understand what happened, but I can encompass it.

Is there a connection to Kabbalistic thought when you stress the incomprehensibility of Auschwitz?

EW: I use mystical signs and symbols when I write. Yet I have not written very much about the connection between traditional concepts and mass murder. In the Kabbalah there is an image named *Zimzum,* which means drawing back. In order to be able to create something God had to draw back. So that we could live, God had to limit himself; otherwise God would not have been able to let his light stream forth. To some extent this also applies to writing about that period. If language is to become a means of communication, one has to draw it back. Such symbols and concepts arise in my writings, but I do not know what the next step is. I could never say that based on Kabbalah I could understand Auschwitz. Never. The farther I get, the less I understand.

INTERRUPTING LANGUAGE: THE EXPERIENCE OF AUSCHWITZ

Language, both religious and literary, was changed by the Shoah. At one point you write that words have lost their innocence after Auschwitz. Forever?

EW: As a Jew, I believe in redemption; that means that nothing stays unclean forever. You can purify what is impure. The Nazis poisoned language; they polluted it. They were masters at finding poetic words for the most hideous things. But language can be restored. Any individual is able to do this whenever writing a different sort of literature and turning words to a different end.

Yes, words have lost their innocence. That is the tragedy. And yet...we must do whatever we can to give words back their innocence, to revivify the purity and dignity of words and in words. Since this event, since Auschwitz, it is hard for me to use certain words. At first I could not even use the word "night." And whenever I see a chimney, I am filled with horror. Does this mean I have to close my eyes? That I cannot do. We do not live in the world only for ourselves, but with ourselves and with others. And language is always a way toward other people.

Language harbors both: positive and negative. Language is dangerous, just as Solomon says in the Bible; life and death depend on language, on words. Each of us can use language for one or the other; each of us can corrupt language or purify it.

In your literary works we find novels and tales as well as essays. Do the essays explain the novels?

EW: Yes, but also the converse: the novels explain the essays. They are all connected; each is part of one and the same mosaic. They all turn on the same pivot which at times remains hidden. My writings complement one another: they complete and cast light on one another, or they stand in a deliberate tension each with the other.

What is at the depths of both the fiction and the essays is the same; what is different is how they reach those depths. I try to reach the same depths, the depths of human existence, of memory, whether with narrative or non-narrative writings, whether with silence or with ideas. They are all a means and a way to strike the chords of memory. With novels and fictional pieces one can reach more readers, but one cannot always stay on the same level. In fiction you move back and forth from lofty flights of ideas to wholly profane, superficial things. For example, the characters say "good morning" to each other, or the story will tell what they had to eat. In essays you do not have to bother with such things. Each sentence has to be rich and meaningful.

Are the questions of characters and persons in your novels your own questions?

EW: Naturally, they all raise my own questions. I am reflected in their situations, playing their roles. Had I found myself in a similar situation, I would have asked their questions. Of course the persons are not simply identical with the author, but the chief characters always have something to do with me myself, not everything, just "something." I'm not talking about the action described in the novels. Not everything that happens to the people in the novels has happened in my life. Nevertheless, there are connections. My main characters are without exception survivors of a Jewish catastrophe, usually the Holocaust, but sometimes a pogrom. Perhaps I myself am that survivor.

Alongside the victims are you also interested in the executioners?

EW: In the eyes of history both belong together: the question of the victims and the question of the executioners who turn them into victims. Both are prisoners of the same situation. I, however, have focused all the attention I can muster exclusively on the fate of the victims. As yet we have not understood them; we have not come closer to them, have not developed enough empathy for them. Therefore, I leave it to others to investigate the psychology of executioners. For myself I am still too much caught up with the victims.

But as many people as have tried to come up with explanations for the event, I do not have any. Whatever can we say looking at Auschwitz? Everything we say is false; whether we say yes or no, it is false. Sometimes all we can do is to weep or to pray, to close our eyes in silent prayer. Any commentary, any interpretation, and especially any explanation, is doomed in advance to fail. Jews and Christians have tried to create a theology from Auschwitz, the way that everything of late gets turned into theology. Others have sketched out a psychology or psychiatry of Auschwitz, even a literature of Auschwitz. They all founder. There can be no novels about Auschwitz.

EW: In contemporary discussions about the meaning of literature, questions about the relationship between ethics and aesthetics always come up. For you, as a strongly ethically motivated writer, how can ethical impulses bear fruit in literature?

EW: Literature's task is to create an ethical awareness. Contemporary literature should not simply please or instruct the reader. On the contrary, it must scratch open the surface, lay bare the wounds and call us to self-reflection and to introspection. That is the task of literature today. It comes down to the search for an ethical frame of mind [*Befindlichkeiten*]. The question is whether what I write helps me make progress in relation to my fellows or not, whether it helps, if not to vanquish evil, at least to alleviate evil's effects. As I have often stressed before, from now on we can no longer say that art is innocent or that literature is innocent. Nothing is innocent anymore. After all that happened fifty years ago even creation itself has lost its innocence. Creativity has lost its innocence too.

   All of these considerations come down to this: We need an ethical perspective in all that we do. It does not mean that we should be continually writing about it. In many of my writings I have tried to make it clear how dangerous it is to be continually writing about Auschwitz. When we do write, however, the memory must be present everywhere, spontaneous and invisible. When a writer is conscious of the memory, keeps it at the back of his mind, he writes differently; then, whether he wants it or not, his writings will have an ethical meaning, an ethical dimension. Even if it is not directly evident, those who interpret literature can find ethical demands in good literature. The reader must find fragments which contain something ethically meaningful, perhaps even against the author's intent. Even if one had to say that this or that were reprehensible, it would still be an ethical message. There is no doubt that the important works of Günter Grass and Heinrich Böll have a powerful ethical content. We do not live in a vacuum and even the writer is caught up in reality. Unless he or she is aware of being connected to what has happened, is happening, and will happen, he or she cannot create a good work of art, since it will lack roots. Today it is only by ethical watchfulness that literature can become a medium which decides—here on the threshold of the next century—between life and death.

In its English version, Adorno's and Horkheimer's book, *Dialektik der Aufklärung*, has the English title, *Eclipse of Reason* [sic].[1] In view of Auschwitz it is not just the eclipse of the sun or the eclipse of God (Buber), but the "eclipse of reason." Do you still put any trust in reason?

EW: We cannot get any further with "pure reason," say, the reason shaped by the Greek philosophers. This has been a bitter discovery for us in this century. Kafka had already foreseen it. Nonetheless, I have trust in human beings. They can, in the course of history, become better persons. Otherwise all our efforts are nothing but an adventure in despair. Human beings have the capacity to be responsible, they have the capacity to know what happened in the past and of what they are capable. If they are aware of the evil they can do, they can also know the good they can do. Without this historical knowledge, without memory, we haven't a chance. But ethical principles only work when we translate them into action. That is what we must try.

There are many sources for ethical behavior. They lie, as I just said, in men, in women, in children, in books, in the past, in memories, yes, in memory above all. The deeper we delve into ourselves, the closer we come to just one of these sources: we discover a source of truth, of love of neighbor. To decide whether what we are doing is good or bad, we have to ask those for whom we are doing it. Others must decide whether the action is good or bad, not I myself. If we are doing something against the will of others, there is no one who knows better whether it is good or bad than those affected by it. The others know your deeds.

Do you have any faith in humankind?

EW: Sometimes. Sometimes I have trust in men and women. Once I gave a guest lecture at the University of Ohio and a student asked me the very same question, whether I believed, as Anne Frank wrote, that all men and women are fundamentally good. I said No! It is a little too simple to say that all men and women are fundamentally good. The difference between Anne Frank and the men and women who shared my experience is that the tragedy began at the point at which Anne Frank's journal ended. What had she seen? She saw her friends and her brother, the cat, the neighbors—good or evil. But the drama began only after she had stopped writing. I would never say that the people in the SS were good people. They weren't at all.

This does not mean that all people are bad. It means that each person is capable of good as well as evil. To say that all people are in principle good would be the same as saying that they are in principle bad. I would like to respect differences and the uniqueness of each person. The Heydrichs and the Eichmanns were human beings. They dehumanized themselves; they lost their humanity. No, they were not good. They were bad and evil.

This turns the problem into a metaphysical one. What has happened to humankind? How can human beings become like this and do something like that? I must confess that I do not know. The only way I can approach—certainly not explain—this reality is that the punishment lies within the crime itself. The dehumanization of the victims—this would be the crime of Eichmann, of Hess and the others. But in doing this they dehumanized themselves; as I said before, they lost their humanity. Perhaps they were good husbands and fathers; but they were no longer human beings.

I once wrote in an essay that in Auschwitz it was man and the idea of man that died, at least for that moment, for that epoch of history. It does not mean that we should not start over again, building up a new humanity. But there is no doubt that at that moment there was nothing but death. Death became the new idol, the new divinity, the new god.

Has anything changed since "the event"?

EW: Yes and no. No, since there are still more than enough people who are inhuman toward other people. You can only judge people according to how they enter into relationship with other people. Being human is not only an ideal, it is a state of being. If I see other people as human beings, this means that I must excuse, or at least understand, their weakness. But being human also takes something more; it takes a certain idealism; it takes kindness, a sensitivity to others, and a certain power of imagination. If these are not present in a person then I have to ask, "You are human and capable of humanity. Why do you not behave that way?" And yet.... Something has changed since the event. So many people are raising their voices against injustice. So many are putting themselves on the side of so many victims, perhaps out of a certain sense of guilt which even many people born afterward have in looking upon the event.

In sum: Things have changed, but not enough. I once naively said that after Auschwitz no war would be thinkable anymore anywhere on earth. After Auschwitz—as I wrote somewhere—I expected the coming of the Messiah, redemption, complete redemption. It did not happen. Today more people die of hunger than ever. As we speak here, a child is dying in Africa. No one can convince me that we are not responsible for that child. For we are among the living, and the child is alive too—and in the blink of an eye the child is dead. This means that we have not learned enough. We must be really determined, and probably humble at the same time. We must demand everything, and be satisfied with the little that we are able to achieve.

How can one change things? By education? By remembrance?

EW: The two are the same: Education occurs through remembrance, and remembrance through education. Education implies remembrance. Without memory we could not study Goethe, Shakespeare, or Plato. Only while remembering Moses, Isaiah, or Buddha can I learn from them. I believe in remembrance more than anything else. I have more trust in education than in the work of politics or in the organized religions. I believe in young people, who are committing themselves, and who in Germany are confronting their past. There must be more and more young Germans who consciously remember Auschwitz—for Germany's sake. If not, the country will run into problems. Perhaps it is already in trouble. It surpasses my understanding that there are politicians who formerly belonged to the SS, that the "historians' debate" has reached such dimensions, or that members of the SS hold yearly meetings. Any individual who has the courage to oppose them brings me hope, and this hope must be strengthened.

How are you involved in the fight against injustice?

EW: Because of what I experienced in Auschwitz, and because nobody stood up for the Jews at that time, I try today to raise my voice wherever men and women are suffering injustice. This means getting involved on the part of Jews in Russia as much as against apartheid in South Africa, against the extermination of Indians in South America and against nuclear war. I even wrote an article on behalf of the Armenians, since I am convinced that we Jews have to stand up on behalf of other men and women. We are obsessed with the idea that being human means sharing our humanity.

And what of human rights in Israel and in the occupied zones? You always stress how much you love Israel.

EW: Yes, I love Israel, which means loving more than the state of Israel, the nation. I mean Israel in a broader sense, I mean Israel's faith, its tradition. When I say that I love Israel it does not mean that I approve of the militarism there. In many places I have publicly protested Israeli incursions. But I try to understand Israel's attitude. The country is surrounded by powers that deny Israel's right to exist, and that spread hatred and destruction. There is no way I would justify many of Israel's actions; I only say that I believe in the Jewish people. There have been times when I loved Israel with pride and with joy. Today I love Israel fearfully.

For me the question of Israel is a very painful one. I do not live in Israel, but, as I just said, I love Israel. I need this love for Israel, which does not mean that I always accept everything that is done there. Many things that happen should not happen. I am more optimistic today than ever before. Things have gotten better since the beginning of the peace talks. We have reached a point of no return. For the first time Israelis and Palestinians are sitting down at one table. They are listening to one another. They are also meeting behind the scenes in order to arrange the scenes, which means they know the other exists, they recognize the other's existence. I am convinced that we are moving toward a new goal, a new understanding. I do not know how it will turn out, but there is no doubt that we are on a path that leads to a change, an official change, a positive change in Israeli-Palestinian relations. And I welcome this change.

AN ETHIC DRAWN FROM MEMORY

Let us talk about Germany. Many are bewildered by the new hatred of foreigners and animosity toward foreigners. How can we respond to this?

EW: If I had the chance to issue an appeal to Germans, particularly to young Germans, then I would say to them: "Never give in to this temptation!" Never let anyone goad you into hating another human being. That is the false path. Hatred is never an answer, never. Hatred destroys the one

who is hated, but it also destroys the one who hates. I myself
was for too long an alien in too many countries not to know
how an alien feels. For many years I was a stateless person.
I never had a passport before I became an American citi-
zen. Wherever I happened to be, I felt unwelcome. Who
wants stateless persons anyway? Everyone is afraid that I,
the stateless person, the refugee, would take away someone's work. And whenever I crossed a border the police and
customs officers would look at me with suspicion. Because
of this I empathize strongly with foreigners, wherever they
are going and wherever they come from. I know that this
causes economic problems, but human problems should
take precedence. I say it again: don't turn away the for-
eigner. Don't give in to those people who say that Germany
must be only for Germans, or France for the French. This is
stupid. Our planet has become a small village. I heard
something very beautiful from one of the space capsules we
sent out.

As an aside, this is one of humankind's most useless
undertakings. There are, I think, two completely useless
organizations. First there are the secret services, the CIA,
KGB, the *Deuxième,* and so on. None of them were able to
predict what happened in Eastern Europe. America has
spent billions and billions of dollars on the CIA. I am sure
that your government also spends millions of marks for
your secret service. None of them were able to predict what
happened, so why should we keep them any longer? We
should take the money and use it to build schools and hos-
pitals, give it to the poor, or do something else with it,
something useful. Second, I have my doubts whether these
space trips are worth the money. I do not know.

Anyway, what I wanted to say was that on one particular
occasion I heard something poetic from a space trip. One
of the astronauts said out there, "From here the planet
looks so small, so very tiny." If it is small, our village, our

house, then we need to keep the doors open. We need to make visitors welcome and make them our friends.

In their fear of foreigners many people distinguish between "economic refugees" and the "really" persecuted. What makes a refugee?

EW: I have a very broad definition of "refugee." Any people who are in such terrible straits where they are living that they do not know how they will be able to feed their children should be accepted as refugees. We should accept them as guests and let them live with us. Naturally, there are political and economic problems if one lets everyone come into a country. But people must take measures against these problems in a timely fashion, by means of education, ideas, and philosophy. Only education can save us. It is precisely here in Germany that people have to be educated. Germany doubtless bears a special responsibility, especially in this century, especially when it comes to foreigners. The slogans of the right-wing parties have to be countered with trust in the majority of the population. And trust in the foreigners. They signify an enrichment of the country where they are accepted. For the most part they bring this country much good; only very infrequently do they cause harm. Pluralism, a diversity of peoples gathered under one roof, is a good thing for Germany. If foreigners are really accepted they will enrich the country where they live.

What do you think about the reunification of Germany today? At first you were very skeptical. Were your fears borne out?

EW: It made me happy to see the Wall fall; yes, I was filled with joy. I saw young people, young people from both sides, embracing one another and drinking champagne. It was a beautiful sign and it made me happy. Not much later I heard the politicians' speeches. Usually when one hears politicians speak it leads to something negative. In particular I heard a very famous politician in Berlin say: "From now on the ninth of November will go down in history." I thought, "My God, has it already been forgotten that the ninth of November went down in history long ago?" The ninth of November was *Kristallnacht.* This means that this victory, the human and democratic victory in Berlin, had overshadowed and eclipsed *Kristallnacht.* This troubled me, for the danger is, could be, that all of this is happening at the price of Jewish remembrance, and that means at the price of remembrance in general.

That is why I voiced some doubts. I must say that I am not at all a man of politics. I don't like to hear too much about politics and I don't pay much attention to the news. I would rather occupy myself with philosophy or literature. They are my passion. People, not politics. However, politics rules our lives. What I do not like is the tone of what is happening in Germany today, in reunified Germany. This has nothing to do with quality of life, but could we not change the tone? I detect a mood of arrogance, not so much among the people, but rather in the government. Something in that troubles me. I hope that most of the young people in Germany speak another language.

Many in Germany, however, say that they do not want to hear about Auschwitz anymore. Constantly remembering stands in the way of reconciliation. Can there ever be reconciliation?

EW: With young Germans there does not need to be any reconciliation at all since there has never been any guilt for them. They are innocent of what happened. The problem for young Germans is to be reconciled with their own past. They need not labor under any feeling of guilt, but rather must feel responsible for what is happening in Germany today, how memory of the past influences the present.

And reconciliation with the other Germans? Well, reconciliation is a concept that must be valid for nations, communities and groups, particularly ethnic and religious groups. Right now, though, we have to be aware that there are many victims who are still alive, and just as many executioners. Therefore, the relationships of the victims to some, I stress some, people in Germany cannot be normal. I myself would not at all want to meet with a captain in the SS. With a general in the army who, let us say, had provided logistical support for the liquidation of the Warsaw ghetto? Well, I would at least have to think about my relationship to him, which means that the relationship is not normal. I would not judge or condemn him. Not I.

As I said before, I do not believe in collective guilt. But just as little do I believe in collective innocence, nor in collective damnation. Perhaps only God could, but not even God does.

There are still people who deny the Holocaust, and others who downplay its significance. How can one confront them?

EW: These people are morally reprehensible, morally sick. Just as there are people who are sick in mind, there are morally sick people too. For myself, I don't even try to understand their ideas, just as all my life I never concerned myself with murderers. My chief concern is with the victims. Why should I waste my time exposing myself to the thinking of the executioners? This is also what I believe about those who deny or downplay Auschwitz. I want to devote myself to the ideas and feelings of the victims. This is why I have never been a Nazi-hunter. Others are fascinated by evil. They ask what made Dr. Mengele into Dr. Mengele. Not I. My life is filled with the tears and the pain of the victims. My field is: What rendered the victims mute when they met Dr. Mengele, what made them cry out, and what drove them into isolation?

You have mentioned the "historians' debate." There are historians who want to integrate the Holocaust into the course of history as a whole.

EW: Yes, they would like to "normalize" the event. This is completely absurd. One cannot repress an event of such magnitude. If it is repressed it reemerges with unbridled power. Germany will be in danger as long as it does not consciously engage its past—psychologically and politically in danger. If an individual person represses a serious event in his life, one day he will find himself on the psychiatrist's couch or in an asylum. Analogously, the same thing can happen to a community.

It turns out that during this debate the German historians never referred to the testimonies of the victims. They used documents of the perpetrators, the Nazis, as the sole basis for their work.

EW: Unfortunately this is true not only of German historians, but of historiography in general. The documents are trusted more than the people who talk about their fate. Even the best historians hold eyewitnesses and journals to be less trustworthy than the naked document. "Document Number XY," authored by anyone at all in Berlin or somewhere else, is more important than a person's memory. One cannot discuss this with historians. I have tried, saying "Look. Facts and the truth are not the same thing." We know the facts, but the truth is something else. One can find it in a journal or in a letter, it may not be a document. Documents report only facts, and facts frequently contradict one another. They are at best a means that help us to find the truth, a truth that might lie in words, in a smile, in a prayer, or in a poem written by a child, or someone face to face with death.

In the historians' debate the uniqueness of the annihilation of the Jews—its singularity—was discussed. Is it possible to get this idea across to others?

EW: I would not want to discourage anyone, but sometimes I think we have lost the struggle for remembrance. This does not mean that we should cease struggling. On the contrary, we must keep on fighting. But time works against us. Joachim Fest said that time is a powerful ally of those who are committed to historicizing National Socialism. People are unwilling to remember. If the truth cannot be lived with, they think, then they could live against the truth. Yet even if there are only a few of us, even if we become steadily fewer, we should still continue to remember. In a hundred years students will find out that there existed a few who stood by their memories. This is reason enough to continue remembering.

It is not easy to explain its uniqueness, or singularity. The oft-repeated argument is still valid: The Jewish people were and are the only people who were marked for complete annihilation. This means that a Jew in the Far East, or a Jew in New York, or in Norway was condemned to death. No other people has shared this fate, outside of a people from antiquity, the Etruscans. They were wiped out, and no one knows why. One day the Romans decided to murder every Etruscan, and then they did it. They went so far as to annihilate the entire culture, and the Etruscan language too. A further reason for the uniqueness of Auschwitz is that no other people was ever as lonely as the Jewish people. During the war other people were oppressed by the Germans besides the Jews. For all of them there were aid and relief committees which supported these peoples. Communists were supported by Moscow, others by Washington or London, but the Jews found no help. No one stood at their side. Even after the war the Jews had no home to return to. If someone from France was freed he returned to his family; even Germans who were in the camps could go back to their homes. The Jews did not know where they could go. If they went back to where they lived before, they would be persecuted, even killed, even after the war. In Hungary, for example, antisemitism was stronger after the war than before, since those who had seized the property of the exiled Jews were unwilling to return anything to the homecomers. The victims had to live through a dual sorrow. Yet all these "rational" arguments aside, there must still be something more, something we are unaware of, that makes the uniqueness so unique.

Does the lack of understanding in so many historians come from the fact that they work with history using scholarly concepts but not with that which Jews understand through memory?

EW: Historians do not take memory as the foundation of their discipline, but only historical facts. They do not even take memory as a methodological presupposition. They frequently turn history against memory. Yet, while memory can certainly get along without knowledge of historical facts, there can never be a science of history without memory. We need a philosophy as the basis for historiography. Contrary to what was considered correct until now, that the discipline of history has to be objective and neutral, I hold that it can be neither objective nor neutral. It needs an ethical perspective. The historian must work from ethical principle; his or her concern must be ethically determined, it must be animated by an ethical passion when researching documents and the fate of men and women. I believe that it is neither possible nor desirable to imagine that a historian could take up this theme, in which there is so much pain and danger, so much darkness and so many flames, without situating it in an ethical context. There must be an historical judgment about what is good and what is wrong, what is evil and what is not.

Is Jewish memory capable of resisting the spirit of the age [Zeitgeist]?

EW: Jewish memory does not resist time, it transcends time. This is a small, but essential distinction. I mean this: resisting time would mean ignoring the time and the events that make up our time. Transcending time means accepting it, taking it up, and passing beyond it in order to attain a comprehensive perspective on time. Jewish memory is something special. Human memory in general is something special, but as a Jew I speak of Jewish memory. Memory wants to bear reality in mind, commemorate it,[2] both the painful and the less painful. Normally, however, memory wants to discard what is painful, it does not want to remember pain. Our bodies, for example, try to overcome pain. If I have a wound it will heal after a short time. Jewish remembrance, on the other hand, wants to recall everything. Choosing what to remember is a moral choice. Fundamental attitudes today are guided by the past, both the distant past as well as the recent past. When I travel in Spain, I run up against what happened there in 1492, just as much as I do something that I am experiencing today. Both are reality. My commitment rises out of that memory, to which new strata are being continually added, through which I pass. Whoever is religious may press back through to the first layer, the memory of God. At a certain point remembering men and women and remembering God flow together.

WRESTLING WITH GOD

The question of God comes up in all your writings, be they stories or articles. Can we talk about God after Auschwitz?

EW: I do not believe that we can talk about God; we can only—as Kafka said—talk to God. It depends on who is talking. What I try to do is speak to God. Even when I speak against God, I speak to God. And even if I am angry at God, I try to show God my anger. But even that is a profession, not a denial of God.

One of the most serious questions I have confronted over the years is whether one can still believe in God after Auschwitz. It was not easy to keep faith. Nevertheless, I can say that, despite all the difficulties and obstacles, I have never abandoned God. I had tremendous problems with God, and still do. Therefore I protest against God. Sometimes I bring God before the bench. Nevertheless, everything I do is done from within faith and not from outside. If one believes in God one can say anything to God. One can be angry at God, one can praise God, one can demand things of God. Above all, one can demand justice of God. As a Jew I place myself within the tradition, the tradition of Moses, Jeremiah, Job, and countless talmudic masters. Like me, they all had difficulties with God. But God also has difficulties with me. I do not think that what I am saying here about my being a Jew, Christians would say about being a Christian. For me, the man that I am, it is possible to be for God with God. It is even possible for me to remain true to myself and be against God, but never without God.

And where is God...?

EW: A great Hassidic master once said: "Where is God? Wherever one lets him in." God is wherever we bring God. We can take God by the hand and show him his friends in the world. We can guide God and show him what is inhuman in men and women. The magnificent idea in our Jewish tradition is that we human beings are responsible for one another. We are also responsible for God. Perhaps that sounds presumptuous but it isn't. It is God's will that we are responsible for God's creation, for God's creatures, and for the creator himself.

In our tradition we say that regarding the Messiah, it is not God who makes the decision. God does not decide when the Messiah comes; we do. When we change the world so that it is ready and worthy, then the Messiah will come. I am convinced that this is the decisive link between human beings and their creator.

This means that only human beings can bring redemption about. I think that this is the difference between the Jewish and Christian traditions. In Christianity, God brings redemption; in Judaism, it is human beings, the individual person. God created the world and it is our task to restore it and redeem it. This gives the individual a tremendous responsibility. Everyone, even the beggar on the street, the porter, the taxi driver, can hasten the coming of the Messiah.

Who is the Messiah in Jewish understanding?

EW: We do not know this, and perhaps we should not know it. There is no image of the Messiah in the Jewish tradition. There is certainly an image of the anti-Messiah, but not of the Messiah. This is so that we do not fall victim to false hopes. We should always wait for the Messiah, for as long as we are waiting, nothing can befall us. While waiting, men and women live together in peace. Problems begin when certain people say that he has already come. That is when civil and religious wars begin. We do not know whether the Messiah is a personal Messiah, a particular person or a time; perhaps he is an epoch. This is all left intentionally in doubt. However all those who believe in the different versions hold one thing in common: we all believe in waiting.

Can there be theology after the event?

EW: Personally I do not think so. There can be no theology after Auschwitz, and no theology whatsoever about Auschwitz. For whatever we do we are lost; whatever we say is inadequate. One can never understand the event with God; one cannot understand the event without God. Theology? The logos of God? Who am I to explain God? Some people try. I think that they fail. Nonetheless, it is their right to attempt it. After Auschwitz everything is an attempt.

God and the death camps. I will never understand that. I try; in every book, every novel, I try something different. There is not one of my books in which I would not try to raise my questions to God's level, which means to ask God what happened and why, why, why. Each ends in failure. I will never understand.

At the beginning of the Yiddish original of your account of Auschwitz you wrote three disturbing sentences: "In the beginning was faith, a naive faith; trust, a false trust; and an illusion, a frightful illusion. We believed in God, we trusted in man and lived in an illusion.... This was the source—if not the reason—for all our misfortune." What do you think about it today?

EW: I stand by this beginning. The words were right, and they are still true today. The source of our misfortune was our faith in God, our being Jews. Our strength became the basis for the destructive power of the executioners. The reason for the Jewish people's suffering was its trust in human beings, who then abused that trust. Faith in God and trust in human beings can no longer be the same today as they were before the event.

You said earlier that after Auschwitz we can no longer do theology. Is telling stories the alternative?

EW: No, it cannot be done instead of theology. Stories help us make some progress with the question of God. But they are not "ersatz theology." I myself tell stories because I love stories and because in my tradition many, many stories are told. Sometimes these stories enter the realm of theology— on a narrative level, that is. Theology is nothing other than telling stories. When you read the Bible you find theology, although in the strict sense the Bible does not do theology.

In the cantata, "I Believe" [*Ani maamin*] you write: "Despite Treblinka. I believe. Because of Belsen. I believe. Because of and despite Majdanek. I believe."

EW: This is a paradox. I deliberately use paradoxical language when it comes to the question of faith after the event. Wherever we turn after Auschwitz we find only despair. If we turn to God we ask ourselves: "How and why can I believe?" If we turn away from God we ask ourselves: "Where can I go?" To human beings? Have human beings earned our trust? And God? No matter in which direction we look we are surrounded by the same dark mystery. And the paradox in this is that despite everything and in defiance of everything we must have faith. Even if we find no faith we must raise it up in the hope that one day we will understand why, and that one day we will be able to give a reason for believing.

How can one combine the struggle with God, which permeates all your work, with ethical maxims? In Christianity the love of God and the love of neighbor cannot be separated; you speak of rebellion against God.

EW: We have to bring the conditions of human existence into our relationship with God. Even when we speak to God, we are not speaking about God, but about human beings. God knows who God is; we do not. Whoever wants to experience more of God must experience more of those whom God has created. However we may never make use of human beings for something, not even in our protest against God.

Perhaps Christians—Muslims too, by the way—cannot understand revolt against God. Perhaps God is too distant for them, a ruler, judge, or father. For us Jews God is a friend. I can argue fiercely with a friend, which does not mean that I reject his friendship. God is present in all that we suppose of him—king, judge, father—but finally, friend. You can see a difference, for example, in the fact that many Christians kneel when praying to God. We Jews stand while we are praying to God. We say, "Look, here we are, we have something to tell you." We have a message for God. What we do in the synagogue is to crown God. We give God a crown as we praise God as the King of the Universe. Abraham Joshua Heschel wrote a book entitled, *God in Search of Man.* God searching for man is a Jewish mystical concept. The *Shekhina,* God's indwelling, means: Something in God longs for human beings. On the other hand, there is a beautiful and very profound notion that a person can say no to God and still be with God, still rely on God.

Recalling your book, *The Six Days of Destruction,* is Auschwitz the anti-creation?

EW: Well, what I tried to do there was to show that the destruction that happened in Auschwitz is analogous to the six days of creation. God is creation; Auschwitz is annihilation. Both are ineffable, incomprehensible, the mystery of mysteries. Auschwitz is innermost to the mystery of God.

And where was God in Auschwitz? Is God a silent God?

EW: When I talk about the silence of God I am thinking of silence on every level, on the human as well as the divine. Either God speaks and we do not hear him, or God does not speak and we only think that God speaks. Which is worse for us? I do not know. But one thing is clear: whatever God does happens by intention; God acts intentionally, and even God's will is wrapped in silence. An old Jewish poet and philosopher, Rabbi Elieser Kalir, once said: "God is not silent. God is silence." Yet God's silence is not that of a passive onlooker. It is a completely different silence. The silence of God is deep and full of meaning. The silence of the onlooker is indifferent, empty; he is not concerned with the other, he is unmoved, impassive, he looks away. Worse still: that silence is self-destructive. Not to see the other, the sufferer, is a sickness. Apathy is a sickness and not just a crime. We can never compare divine silence with human silence.

In the Midrash there is a story that God sheds two tears when a person dies. They fall in the ocean and make a sound that can be heard from one end of the horizon to the other. And in Auschwitz? Where was God in Auschwitz? Were we unable to hear God's tears because we ourselves have not wept enough?

Does this mean that God is a suffering God? Is God weak, as Dietrich Bonhoeffer wrote, so that it is not a stronger, but rather a weaker God, one who suffers, who can help us?

EW: I am not convinced of that, since it contradicts the Jewish tradition. We do not believe in a weak God. God is the king of the universe, God is strong and omnipotent. God could do whatever God wants. But God does not. Should we feel compassion for God, not because God is weak, but because we abuse God's work. We destroy the world, God's creation. We break the trust that God placed in us.

That God suffers with us is no sign of weakness. Perhaps it is melancholy, perhaps longing, perhaps loneliness—but not weakness. If God wanted he could bring the course of things to a halt and turn everything on its head. God could take away the murderer's strength and the victim's weakness. God does not do this, since God has God's reasons. We do not know. We have to live with the question of why God does not do it.

God's loneliness—what does that mean?

EW: God, only God, is alone. By definition. Human beings are not alone. They have other human beings. But whom does God have? God is condemned to be alone. It is true that God has us, but this is not the same. We human beings are not God. What I am thinking of here is God's tragedy. If a human being no longer wants to live, he or she commits suicide. God cannot kill himself. Therefore we should have sympathy for God, compassion for God. This is an old Hassidic idea: compassion for God.

Does God's loneliness have to do with the loneliness of the human person?

EW: I do not think so. God has created us in God's image, as the Bible says. But does this mean that we are as lonely as God? Naturally, there are moments of loneliness in our lives. Human existence expresses a certain loneliness. Even if one is very close to another person, even if one loves him or her, loneliness still looms on the horizon. At some point we will lose the one we love—through death, for instance— or the other will lose us. Loneliness surrounds us human beings, but it is never as total as the loneliness of God.

Negative images of God can also be found in your writings. For example, you sometimes speak of the madness of God.

EW: The madness of God means that our understanding of God can be filled with madness. It does not mean that God is mad. We project our madness onto God. But look, all of these are only attempts, possible stances; they are only questions, complete with a question mark. I do not know the answer. As I said, in every book I try a different approach. I turn around and open this door. Perhaps the answer is here. I open the next door; perhaps the answer lies there. And there are so many doors.

The approaches you point to often sound paradoxical. Can we only approach God by way of paradox?

EW: No, I think that we can only approach God in simplicity. Only the path of simplicity leads to God. When things get complicated and complex we separate ourselves from God. And here I am one with the Hassidic tradition in the conviction that the simplest path to God passes through other people. One person alone is not close to God. In order to be close to God that person must be close to another person. There are many ways of relating to other people. Some are complicated, painful, full of pretense and suffering—but God does not dwell there. God does not love the complex, but the simple.

I am absolutely convinced that God is to be found in a simple human relationship. We have few certainties, but this is one of them: When two people love one another, God is there. God is present when people are present to and for one another in a human way. God does not say "Your life belongs to me." God says, "Your life belongs to your neighbor."

May I ask something further about the Jewish-Christian dialogue? In view of Auschwitz, what are the most important tasks for Christians? I know that this is not your problem.

EW: It is our problem, and therefore mine too. I once said (and I shocked many Christians in so doing) that "The victims are my problem; the murderers are yours." But despite this, since these are human questions they naturally concern me to some extent. I think that Christians have to try to understand what has happened to the Christian tradition. After all, Christianity is a religion of love. What happened to love? Why throughout history was everything Jewish rejected? And then this question: How has Christianity contributed in some way to Auschwitz?

Let me give you an example. On the first night I arrived in the camp the image I had before my eyes was the image of the Inquisition, fire, the persecution of the Jews in the Middle Ages. I remembered my childhood. In our home we had a "Jewish Encyclopedia" in which a picture of the Inquisition and the persecution of the Jews was printed. Jews were burned at the stake then. What was going on? Were such horrible things a sort of preview, a premonition of what was to come, even if to an unimaginably greater degree? Why were the Jews abandoned by so many Christians?

Nonetheless, Christians should not develop feelings of guilt. If other Christians have failed with respect to the Jews, you should not despair in Christianity. You should not come to the conclusion that you should abandon Christianity. Try to find the truth within your tradition and within your faith. Transform Christianity and help others to transform it.

When Christians talk about Auschwitz they always run the danger of wanting to give meaning to the suffering of the Jews, and, what is worse, a Christological meaning.

EW: This is absolutely false. Christians must never interpret Auschwitz Christologically. Even Pope John Paul II runs this danger. After a visit to the concentration camp at Mauthausen, for example, he said that the Holocaust is a gift to humanity. That is too insensitive. It would mean that we should thank God for the gift. This is impossible; these are wrong words. Perhaps one could say that Auschwitz is a lesson, but never a gift. Later I spoke with Cardinal Lustiger, the Bishop of Paris, and he said: "Look, a Christological concept is hidden there. Jesus' death is interpreted as a gift to humanity. And because of this one comes to see the death of the Jews likewise as a gift." No, death is never a gift. The Jewish tradition would never accept this idea. Life is a gift, but not death.

Do you think that it is possible to purify the Christian tradition of the traces of anti-Judaism.

EW: I am convinced of it. Anti-Judaism is not rooted at the center of Christian doctrine, but it was often present in Christianity's traditions. Reading what some of the Fathers of the Church—Chrysostom, for example—say about the Jews, you can only be filled with horror. Or recall Luther's later anti-Jewish attitude. But today there are many positive signs.

Here again let me give an example: Once I was invited to a university in Ohio. It was called "Wittenberg University," a Lutheran college. There were some two thousand students and professors there. After my lecture the President conferred on me an honorary doctorate. He said, "I confer this distinction on you with a deep sense of regret for Luther's anti-Semitism." He said this publicly, in the presence of all the students and teachers. Something like this shows courage and integrity, and I am grateful for it.

One question in conclusion: Do God and humanity have a chance for a future?

EW: God is God. Having said this I have said everything. Everything else comes after that, for God is God. But what does this mean for humanity's fate? For the world? For death? For evil? If God is everywhere, then he is everywhere. If you believe in God (and if not I respect you just as much) then you have to say at the end, as in the beginning: God is God.

Today all of us are living in biblical times. Everything is going so quickly. The many events of recent times have increased the pace even more. We have the feeling that this century, which, as Hannah Arendt said, is the cruelest century of recorded history, wants to shed its cruelty, its outbreaks of hate and murder, its outpouring of blood. And because of this we have the feeling that our planet is outstripping us, that history is racing toward the year 2000. In the year 2000 everything will change, and you, the young generation, will be responsible for this change.

Believe me, I place a great deal of hope on the shoulders of the younger generation—everywhere, but in Germany too. You have to justify the trust I have in you. This is your work.

The most important thing that we can learn from one another is to be faithful to the truth, and that while the truth is one, there are many ways that lead to it. A Jew is not better than you, or worse. A Jew is not more faithful to the truth than you, or less righteous. A Jew is just like you: lost in a world in which he or she searches in despair for the meaning of his or her existence. And while we are here for this brief journey, we ought to help one another and be human toward one another instead of fighting each other.

There is a wonderful story, an old legend which I have traced back to its talmudic sources. A king heard that there lived in his kingdom a wise man who spoke every language in the world. He could listen to the twittering birds and understand their songs. He could read the shapes of the clouds and grasp their meaning. He could also read others' thoughts. The king sent someone to the wise man to bring him to his palace. The wise man came.

Then the king said to him: "Is it true that you know every language?"

"Yes, majesty."

"Can you really listen to the birds and understand their songs?"

"Yes, majesty."

"And is it true that you understand the language of the clouds?"

"Yes majesty."

"Is it true that you can read other people's thoughts?"

"Yes majesty."

Then the king said, "Behind my back I am holding a bird in my hands. Tell me, is it alive or is it dead?"

The wise man became anxious, for he sensed that whatever he said the king could kill the bird. He looked at the king and was silent for a long time. Finally he said something that I would also like to say to my readers:

"The answer, your majesty, lies in your hand."

You have asked about the future. The answer lies in our hands.

Notes

1. [The English of *Dialektic der Aufklärung* is *Dialectic of Enlightenment,* translated by John Cumming (New York: Herder and Herder, 1972). *The Eclipse of Reason* (New York: Continuum, 1974), was written later, in English, by Horkheimer alone.—*trans.*]

2. [The German verb used is *gedenken,* which means to remember or to bear in mind, but, also, to commemorate.—*trans.*]

SUGGESTED READINGS BY ELIE WIESEL[†]

Night. The original version appeared in Yiddish: *Un di Welt hot geschwign.* Buenos Aires, 1956. A reworked and abbreviated version, *La Nuit* (1958), appeared as *Night,* translated by Stella Rodway with a foreword by François Mauriac. New York: Hill and Wang, 1960. *Wiesel's autobiographical account of his time in the camps at Auschwitz and Buchenwald.*

Novels

Town Beyond the Wall, translated by Stephen Becker. New York: Athenaeum, 1964. *This book marks a turning point in Wiesel's work, with a much stronger retrieval of Jewish traditions. Relationships and friendships between the characters become possible for the first time in a novel. The important leitmotifs of his work announce themselves: silence, madness, indifference and struggling with God.*

A Beggar in Jerusalem, translated by Lily Edelman and Elie Wiesel. New York: Random House, 1970. *The action of this novel unfolds in a more difficult and involved way. Several features of this novel are characteristic of Wiesel's experimental style. Individual scenes fit together like pieces in a mosaic. Past and present interpenetrate one another. The beggars are messengers; Jerusalem is the city in which the Jewish destiny is reflected.*

[†] (English editions of the German works cited have been given where I have been able to find them. Since the originals were not written in German, I have not included the German texts cited in *Trotzdem hoffen.* Once again, the annotations are the work of interviewers.—*trans.*)

The Oath, translated by Marion Wiesel. New York: Random House, 1973. *The central question of whether it is at all possible to grasp the experience of the annihilation of the Jews in speech is worked out narratively in this book. At its center stand the leitmotifs of silence and passion for life.*

The Fifth Son, translated by Marion Wiesel. New York: Random House, 1985. *The importance in Judaism of remembering and of telling stories encounters its limits in the face of the Shoah. The survivors are unable to communicate to their children what they had to go through. These children, some of whom took up their careers again in postwar Germany, experience it nonetheless, giving rise to the idea of vengeance–against the murders.*

The Forgotten, translated by Stephen Becker. New York: Summit Books, 1985. *Individuals can fall victim to the season of forgetting; collectives can as well. Who is the bearer of memory when forgetfulness takes hold?*

Biblical, Talmudic and Hassidic Works

Souls on Fire: Portraits and Legends of Hasidic Masters, translated by Marion Wiesel. New York: Random House, 1972. *The great Hasidic Masters, their deeds and stories, as well as the legends that surround them are forcefully retold here. This book could very well stand as an introduction to the hasidic strand of Judaism.*

Adam oder Das Geheimnis des Anfangs (1975), Freiburg, 1987. *The biblical figures are our contemporaries. Their fate and their message concern today's men and women. Wiesel tries to get in touch with them, "reaching across the abyss."*

Die Weisheit des Talmud. Geschichten und Porträts (1991), Freiburg, 1992. *Whoever wants to understand the Jewish religion must know the Talmud. Here Wiesel undertakes a broadranging journey through the intricate and fascinating paths of the Talmud.*

Dramas and Essays

The Trial of God (as it was held on February 25, 1649 in Shamgorod): A Play in Three Acts, translated by Marion Wiesel. New York: Random House, 1979. *One of his most theologically explosive works. God is put on trial for cruelty and indifference in the face of the fate of the Jews. Who is willing to defend God?*

Legends of Our Time. New York: Rinehart and Winston, 1968. *The earliest and most important of Wiesel's essays and stories. The whole book is a plea on behalf of the victims of Auschwitz.*

From the Kingdom of Memory: Reminiscences. New York: Summit Books, 1990. *A collection of more recent essays on memory and ethics, on the problem of hatred and on the struggle for human rights.*

With Albert Friedlander, *The Six Days of Destruction: Meditations toward Hope.* Mahwah, N.J.: Paulist Press, 1988. *Stories about the suffering of the Shoah and suggestions for how memory can be culturally and religiously preserved–for the sake of the future.*

Eugene J. Fisher and Leon Klenicki, editors, *In Our Time: The Flowering of Jewish-Catholic Dialogue* (A Stimulus Book, 1990).

Leon Klenicki, editor, *Toward A Theological Encounter* (A Stimulus Book, 1991).

David Burrell and Yehezkel Landau, editors, *Voices from Jerusalem* (A Stimulus Book, 1991).

John Rousmaniere, *A Bridge to Dialogue: The Story of Jewish-Christian Relations;* edited by James A. Carpenter and Leon Klenicki (A Stimulus Book, 1991).

Michael E. Lodahl, *Shekhinah/Spirit* (A Stimulus Book, 1992).

George M. Smiga, *Pain and Polemic: Anti-Judaism in the Gospels* (A Stimulus Book, 1992).

Eugene J. Fisher, editor, *Interwoven Destinies: Jews and Christians Through the Ages* (A Stimulus Book, 1993).

Anthony Kenny, *Catholics, Jews and the State of Israel* (A Stimulus Book, 1993).

Eugene J. Fisher, editor, *Visions of the Other: Jewish and Christian Theologians Assess the Dialogue* (A Stimulus Book, 1995).

Leon Klenicki and Geoffrey Wigoder, editors, *A Dictionary of the Jewish-Christian Dialogue* (Expanded Edition), (A Stimulus Book, 1995).

Frank E. Eakin, Jr. *What Price Prejudice?: Christian Antisemitism in America* (A Stimulus Book, 1998).

STIMULUS BOOKS are developed by Stimulus Foundation, a not-for-profit organization, and are published by Paulist Press. The Foundation wishes to further the publication of scholarly books on Jewish and Christian topics that are of importance to Judaism and Christianity.

Stimulus Foundation was established by an erstwhile refugee from Nazi Germany who intends to contribute with these publications to the improvement of communication between Jews and Christians.

Books for publication in this Series will be selected by a committee of the Foundation, and offers of manuscripts and works in progress should be addressed to:

Stimulus Foundation
c/o Paulist Press
997 Macarthur Boulevard
Mahwah, N.J. 07430